Reading Activities A to Z

Joanne Matricardi
Jeanne McLarty

THOMSON

DELMAR LEARNING   Australia Brazil Canada Mexico Singapore Spain United Kingdom United States

THOMSON
DELMAR LEARNING

Reading Activities A to Z
Joanne Matricardi and Jeanne McLarty

Vice President, Career Education Strategic Business Unit:
Dawn Gerrain

Director of Learning Solutions:
John Fedor

Managing Editor:
Robert L. Serenka, Jr.

Senior Acquisitions Editor:
Erin O'Connor

Product Manager:
Philip Mandl

Editorial Assistant:
Alison Archambault

Director of Production:
Wendy A. Troeger

Production Manager:
Mark Bernard

Content Project Manager:
Karin Hillen Jaquays

Technology Project Manager:
Sandy Charette

Director of Marketing:
Wendy E. Mapstone

Channel Manager:
Kristin McNary

Marketing Coordinator:
Scott A. Chrysler

Marketing Specialist:
Erica S. Conley

Art Director:
Joy Kocsis

Cover Design:
Joseph Villanova

Any additional questions about permissions can be submitted by email to thomsonrights@thomson.com

Library of Congress Cataloging-in-Publication Data

Matricardi, Joanne.
  Reading activities A to Z / Joanne Matricardi and Jeanne McLarty.
    p. cm.
  Includes bibliographical references and index.
  ISBN-13 978-1-4180-4852-5
  ISBN-10 1-4180-4852-6
  (alk. paper)
  1. Reading (Early childhood)—Activity programs.
2. Reading readiness.
I. McLarty, Jeanne. II. Title.
  LB1139.5.R43M28 2007
  372.4—dc22

2007006508

NOTICE TO THE READER

Publisher does not warrant or guarantee any of the products described herein or perform any independent analysis in connection with any of the product information contained herein. Publisher does not assume, and expressly disclaims, any obligation to obtain and include information other than that provided to it by the manufacturer.

The reader is expressly warned to consider and adopt all safety precautions that might be indicated by the activities herein and to avoid all potential hazards. By following the instructions contained herein, the reader willingly assumes all risks in connection with such instructions.

The Publisher makes no representation or warranties of any kind, including but not limited to, the warranties of fitness for particular purpose or merchantability, nor are any such representations implied with respect to the material set forth herein, and the publisher takes no responsibility with respect to such material. The Publisher shall not be liable for any special, consequential, or exemplary damages resulting, in whole or part, from the readers' use of, or reliance upon, this material.

Contents

Preface

A child's success in reading is related to the value placed on reading by the people close to the child. Traditionally this means the family, but it should be expanded to include caregivers and teachers. An appreciation of literacy is developed by seeing adults read, having adults read to the child, and having reading material available.

The ability to read is developed in stages (see Table 1). Each stage is important but not all-inclusive. Children learn best when all components are integrated and given repetitive practice. This practice must be varied through different types and styles of activities to accommodate children's interests and learning needs. The activities presented in *Reading Activities A to Z* are predominately pre-reading skills. The book's goal is to help parents, teachers, and student teachers get children ready to read.

Reading is usually introduced as a formal unit of instruction in kindergarten or first grade. The later stages of fluency and comprehension are found here. Some four-year-olds will be ready to recognize simple words and start to develop a sight word vocabulary. According to the National Institute of Child Health and Human Development, preschoolers should be encouraged to "learn the letters of the alphabet, to discriminate letters from one another, to print letters, and to attempt to spell words that they hear" (Lyon, 1998, ¶38).

Phonemic awareness is an integral part of the pre-reading experience. A phoneme is the smallest unit of sound in a spoken word. Phonemic awareness is the ability to identify sounds in words. "Phonemic awareness instruction might be thought of as prephonics or phonics without printed letters" (Smith & Read, 2005, p. 48). Phonics is the understanding of the relationship between phonemes and graphemes—letters that represent those sounds in written language. The graphemes may be individual such as the |a| in apple, or it may be a blend, such as the |ch| in catch.

Print awareness is a bridge between phonemic awareness and phonics. Children need to see words written in association with objects or songs before they are able to read. Print awareness begins with the recognition that marks on paper represent words. This will expand into identifying and writing alphabet letters.

Reading Activities A to Z also includes prewriting activities. The ability to write accompanies the ability to read. "Reading (decoding) and writing (encoding) should be developed jointly whenever possible. They are mutually reinforcing activities" (Emery, 1975, p. 59). The reading and pre-reading skills, along with writing, are listed in an index, with a list of activities reinforcing these skills.

Reading Activities A to Z presents activities in an alphabetical layout. This provides an easy

Table 1 Stages and Scope of Reading Skills

Stages of Reading Skills	Scope of Reading Skills
Develop appreciation of literacy	Language rich environment
	Speak and read to children
	Listening ability
	Presence of reading material
	Model reading
	Develop vocabulary
Phonemic Awareness	Understanding and identifying the individual units of sounds in words
	Rhyming and alliteration
Print Awareness	Recognition that marks on paper represent words
	Recognition of letters
	Visual discrimination
	Left to right progression
Phonics	Understanding the relationship between phonemes (sounds) and graphemes (letters that represent sounds)
	Decoding—ability to break written word into sequence of sounds
Fluency	Ability to recognize words quickly
	Develop sight vocabulary
Comprehension	Understanding what is read

way for reading activities to highlight a particular letter. The activities are presented in a lesson plan format. There are seven areas: "Developmental Goals," "Skill Explanation," "Learning Objective," "Materials," "Adult Preparation," "Activity Introduction Suggestion," and "Procedures." The developmental goals offer social-emotional, physical, and cognitive concepts to be explored. Skill explanation addresses the reason the activity is pre-reading or reading. The learning objective states what the children will use to accomplish the immediate goal of the lesson. The materials section presents all that is required from the preparation through the implementation of the activity. The activity introduction suggestion gives an aid to help motivate children. Adults may quote this section, put it in their own words, or create an entirely new introduction. It is not meant to stifle creativity, but only offered as one way to get the children started. The procedures section involves a step-by-step process for the child to successfully accomplish the lesson.

Age appropriateness for activities is given. This is just a suggestion. Knowing the children's abilities and attention span will help determine what activities may be done and whether or not they need to be altered.

Many of the activities lend themselves to a theme. For those activities, a theme suggestion introduction is also given. However, activities that are ongoing do not have a theme. An example of this is the Sign-in Board. Children are responsible for their own attendance each day. No theme is needed.

Most activities have a book suggestion. These are common books found at our local public library. The value of reading to children on a daily basis cannot be emphasized enough. The adult must select books that he or she enjoys. Enthusiasm for reading will transfer to the children.

Additional sections for activities may be "Notes," "Variation," or "Safety Precaution." Notes offers further clarification. A variation may be given for an alternate theme or to change the activity for a different age child. Safety precautions are offered when closer supervision or alertness is needed.

Some of the lessons include the use of patterns in the creation of materials. All suggested patterns are located in the Appendix. The patterns are not meant to use only one time. Materials should be carefully created and preserved for future service. The "Helpful Hints" section of this book contains suggestions for material preservation.

Activities are presented in this book may involve large muscles. This is known as kinesthetic involvement, which promotes retention. Cross-lateral movement also enhances learning. The left side of the brain controls the right side of the body. Conversely, the right side of the brain controls the left side of the body. When both sides of the brain are involved, problem-solving abilities are strengthened (Jensen, 2004). In the activity *Obstacle Course*, children identify alphabet letters when crawling through an obstacle course, (the right arm moves with the left leg, and the left arm moves with the right arm). Both sides of the brain will be engaged. Retention and retrieval of this knowledge will be greater.

Creating food through the use of rebus recipes is offered in *Doggie, Doggie, Where's Your Bone?, Frozen Fruit Pops, Toast Writing, and Wild Thing Snack*. Please note the safety suggestions and closely supervise children to avoid the danger of choking. Another consideration is to always check for any food allergies before beginning a food activity.

An Online Companion resource located at http://www.earlychilded.delmar.com is an accompaniment to *Reading Activities A to Z*. This site contains additional group activities for young children. The activities are written in the same lesson plan format found in this book. These detailed plans include developmental goals, skill explanation, learning objectives, a list of materials, directions for adult preparation, activity introduction suggestion, and a step-by-step procedure for the child. The activities are easy to understand and implement, either in the preschool classroom or at home. The *Reading Activities A to Z* online resource also provides links to related preschool sites. These links contain additional ideas, patterns, book sources, and other reading and pre-reading materials.

ACKNOWLEDGMENTS

This book is an accumulation of original and shared ideas developed over 45 years of teaching young children. We would like to thank our co-workers, students, and their parents for sharing and experimenting with us. We, and the editors at Thomson Delmar Learning, would also like to thank the following reviewers for their time, effort, and thoughtful contributions which helped to shape the final text:

Christine Pieper, MA
Director of Program Development
Petaluma, CA

Katherine M. Lozano
Executive Director Blessed Sacrament Academy
Child Development Center San Antonio, TX

Jennifer M. Johnson, BS, M.Ed.
Early Childhood Program Head
Vance Granville Community College,
North Carolina

Joni Levine M.Ed.
Community College of Allegheny County,
Pennsylvania

Patricia Capistron
Lead Teacher
Rocking Unicorn Nursery School in Chatham,
Massachusetts

Marilyn Rice, M.Ed.
Director: Curriculum and Training
Tuckaway Child Development Center, Virginia

Lynnette McCarty
Executive Director/Owner
Serendipity Children's Center, Washington
President-The National Association of
Childcare Professionals

Wendy Bertoli
Early Childhood Education Instructor
Lancaster County Career and Technology
Center, Pennsylvania

HELPFUL HINTS

Throughout the years we've developed strategies which have helped our activities to proceed more smoothly. Some are specific to reading and writing, others may deal with behavior management techniques or the preservation of materials so that they may be used year after year. The following helpful hints have become routine in our classrooms.

Specific to Reading and Writing

✄ When writing, children need to write on the same plane. Writing on a table—the sample needs to be on the table. Writing on a board—the sample needs to be on a board.

✄ Use lowercase letters with the children whenever possible. Typically, children

recognize uppercase letters first. Perhaps this is because many adults have a tendency to write in capitals when they print.

✄ Use the same colors within each word when writing for children. If the colors vary, the eye will jump from color to color and not see the word as a whole.

✄ Write with dark-colored markers. Yellow, orange, and pink are too difficult to see.

✄ Often the activities ask the adult to put some of the pieces in a basket. If a small basket is unavailable, use a gift bag.

✄ Create a print-rich environment by placing words around the room near permanent objects such as the *sink, door, mirror,* etc.

Behavior Management Techniques

✄ The most important aspect of working with young children is that the adults enjoy the activity. Enthusiasm is contagious. Conversely, simply going through the motions of an activity will be noticeable by the children, and their actions will reflect the adult's attitude.

✄ Be prepared. When it is time to start an activity, you should already have all the materials you need. Children will not sit still waiting for you to get ready.

✄ Maintain eye contact with the children. This helps them to sit for longer periods and keeps them interested in the activity.

✄ When reading a book, hold the book open as you read so children can see the pictures. Know the material well enough that you can comfortably glance away from the text. It is important to spend more time looking at the children than looking at the words.

✄ Always keep the group's age and attention span in mind when planning activities. Be flexible. A group activity may need to be cut short if the attention is waning.

✄ Alternate quiet and active activities. Too many quiet plans may cause the children to lose interest. Too many active ones many cause them to become overstimulated.

Preservation of Materials

✂ When creating materials, use rubber cement for gluing; white glue may cause paper to wrinkle.

✂ If possible, laminate all materials made with paper. A laminator may be purchased for anywhere between $350 and $1500. Some school supply or office supply stores will laminate materials for a set fee.

✂ If you do not have access to a laminator, use clear, unpatterned contact paper or heavy tag board.

✂ Store materials in resealable plastic bags. This allows you to see at a glance what is inside, and makes storage in a filing cabinet or file box easier. Before using plastic bags, check with the school's policies. Some centers are not allowed to use plastic bags. Envelopes or folders may be used in place of the resealable plastic bags.

SUPPLIES NEEDED

Most early childhood programs operate on a limited budget. Many of the materials we use in this book may be purchased at your local dollar store. The shopping list that follows has been divided into five categories: consumables, non-consumables, equipment, kitchen equipment, and recyclable items. Also included in the Appendix are Family Letters requesting specific items.

CONSUMABLE

Aluminum foil
Blank audio tape
Broad-tipped markers
Camera and film
Carbon paper
Card stock paper
Chart tablet
Clear contact paper
Colored pencils
Coloring book
Composition book
Construction paper (assorted colors and sizes)
Copy paper
Cotton swabs
Crayons
Envelopes
File folders
Fine-tipped markers
Foam pieces
Foam sheets
Heavyweight string
Hook and loop tape
Hot glue gun sticks
Index cards (assorted sizes)
Journal
Kazoos
Large paper
Liquid watercolor
Lower case alphabet strip
Magnetic tape (self-sticking)
Masking tape
Mat
Notebook paper
Paint brushes (new and narrow)
Paper clips (metal)
Paper plates
Paper towels
Pencils
Pens
Permanent markers
Permanent markers (fine-tipped)
Plastic cups (assorted sizes)
Plastic knives
Plastic tablecloth
Poster board
Quills
Removable stickers
Resealable plastic bag—gallon size
Resealable plastic bags—quart size
Resealable plastic bags—sandwich size
Rubber cement
Sand
Sandpaper
Shaving cream
Snap clothespins
Staples
String
Tag board
Tempera paint (assorted colors)
Three-prong folder
Unlined paper
Washable finger paint
Washable markers
White school glue
Window markers
Yarn

NON-CONSUMABLE

54" square vinyl tablecloth
Adult scissors
Alphabet stamps
Baskets (assorted sizes)
Bell
Blanket
Blocks
Blond-haired doll
Book bag
Candlestick
Child-size safety scissors
Child-size umbrella
Clipboard
Doll with hair
Hole punch
Hot glue gun
Ice cube tray
Large plastic tub
Mallet for xylophone
Magnetic wand
Metal rings (2")
Mirror
Pet toys
Pitcher
Plastic eggs
Plastic jar
Plastic sunglasses
Plastic zoo animals
Rocks
Rope tied in knot
Ruler
Small ball
Small pail
Small paint brushes
Smocks
Spoons
Squeeze bottles
Stapler
Stuffed animal
Stuffed toy bears (small, medium & large)
Suitcase
Tape measure
Toy car

Toy chairs (small, medium, large)
Toy moon
Toy star
Toy xylophone
Trays
Wordless picture books
Yardstick

EQUIPMENT
Bean bags
Camera
Chairs
Digital camera
Dry erase board
Flannel board
Full length mirror
Large plastic container

Record player
Small plastic container
Sensory table
Tables
Tape recorder
Wooden blocks (small, medium, large)

KITCHEN EQUIPMENT
Baking sheet
Bowls (assorted sizes)
Colander
Cutting board
Measuring cups
Measuring spoons
Mixing spoon
Pitcher

RECYCLABLE ITEMS
Advertisements
Baseball hats
Comics from newspaper
Computer keyboard
Containers
Labels from cans, boxes, or bags
Large buttons
Large paper grocery bags
Magazines
Milk caps
Newspapers
Paper towel tubes
Shoe boxes
Shopping bag
Small box
Stick or pole

FOOD
Beef broth (15 oz. can)
Flour
Food coloring
Fruit cocktail (15 oz. can)
Grapes
Lemon juice
Milk
Rice cakes
Salt
Shredded cheese
Sliced bread
Strawberries
Unsweetened applesauce
Whipped cream cheese

KEY TERMS FOR READING AND READING READINESS

Comprehension:	The ability to read and understand what is being read
Decoding:	The ability to break a written word into a sequence of sounds, thus sounding out a word
Dolch word list:	Two hundred and twenty words that are listed in order of their frequency of use
Fluency	The ability to recognize a word quickly
Graphemes	A single letter or a group of letters that represent sounds
High frequency words	Words that are used most often
Phonemes	The smallest unit of sound in a spoken word
Phonemic awareness	Understanding and identifying the small units of sound in words
Phonics	Understanding the relationship between phonemes and graphemes
Sight words	Words that are identified by merely looking at them rather than decoding them

READING AND PRE-READING SKILLS INDEX

DEVELOP APPRECIATION OF LITERACY
Bear Bag Story
Book Buddies
Class Books
Do You Hear What I Hear?
Doggie, Doggie, Where's Your Bone?
Newspaper Letter Hunt
Traveling Pet
Umbrella Story Starter
Wordless Picture Books
Zipper Bag Story

LISTENING SKILLS
Clothesline Story
Family Book
Flexible Flannel Board Stories
Interview
Great Gruff Goats' Position Words
Job Dictation
Predicting an Outcome
Queen's Crown
Yeniel the Yak
Zoo Adventures

DEVELOP VOCABULARY
Dandy Dictionary
Great Gruff Goats' Position Words

PHONEMIC AWARENESS
Collage
Endless Ending Sounds
Ice Skating
Nursery Rhymes
Portfolio of Stories
Queen's Crown
Vowel Song
Yeniel the Yak

PRINT AWARENESS
Class Books
Do You Hear What I Hear?
Family Book
Finger Paint Writing
Great Gruff Goats' Position Words
Ice Pop Writing
Interview
Job Dictation
Label Match
Outdoor Writing
Predicting an Outcome
Rebus Books
Song Board Singing
Traveling Pet
Umbrella Story Starter
Under the Table Writing
Yeniel the Yak
Zoo Adventures

ALPHABET RECOGNITION
Air Writing
Alligator Alphabet Puzzle
Alphabet Children
Ants Go Marching through the Alphabet
Egg Word Creations
Finger Paint Writing
Head Band of Letters and Pictures
Keyboard Match
Letter Bag
Mirror Writing
Newspaper Letter Hunt
Obstacle Letter Search
Quill Writing
Stamp Name Game
Tracing Letters
Underwater Letter Match
X-Ray Vision
Xylophone Letter Match

LEFT-TO-RIGHT PROGRESSION
Alligator Alphabet Puzzle
Doggie, Doggie, Where's Your Bone?
Frozen Fruit Pops
Growing Up Picture Strip

VISUAL DISCRIMINATION
Ants Go Marching through the Alphabet
Classmate Bingo
Clothesline Story
Hide and Seek High Frequency Words
Jigsaw Puzzle
Key Words
Kite Visual Discrimination
Magnetic Word Match
Trademark Match
Underwater Letter Match
Vehicle Word Match

PRE-WRITING AND WRITING
Air Writing
Everlasting Puffy Paint
    Words
Finger Paint Writing
Ice Pop Writing
Journals
Lemon Juice Writing
Magic Names
Mirror Writing
Portfolio of Stories
Quill Writing
Record Writing
Roller Bottle Writing
Shaving Cream Writing
Sign-in Board
Toast Writing
Traveling Pet
Under the Table Writing
Yarn Words

PHONICS
Collage
Egg Word Creations
Endless Ending Sounds
Headband of Letters
    and Pictures
Journals
Letter Bag
Portfolio of Stories

FLUENCY
Building Sentences
    with Friends
Classmate Bingo
Color Words
Dandy Dictionary
Everlasting Puffy Paint
    Words
Fishy Words
Hide and Seek High
    Frequency Words
Jigsaw Puzzle
Jump Words
Key Words
Magic Names
Magnetic Word
    Match
Number Word
    Recognition
Portfolio of Stories
Queen's Crown
Quill Writing
Rebus Books
Sign-in Board
Shaving Cream
    Writing
Stamp Name
    Game
Vocabulary Building
    Blocks
Worm Word Search
Yarn Words

COMPREHENSION
Building Sentences
    with Friends
Color Words
Number Word
    Recognition
Portfolio of Stories

Air Writing

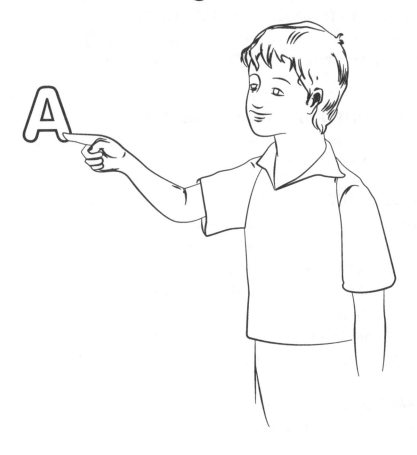

AGES: 3–6

GROUP SIZE:
2–4 children

DEVELOPMENTAL GOALS:
- ✂ To identify alphabet letters
- ✂ To practice pre-writing skills

LEARNING OBJECTIVE:
Using letter cards, the children will recognize and practice writing the letter.

MATERIALS:
5" × 7" unlined index cards
Broad-tipped marker
Basket
Samples of writing styles (Appendix C)

SKILL EXPLANATION:

Air writing is a prelude to writing on paper. Writing and reading complement each other in the learning process. This activity also involves identifying alphabet letters, which is a step involved in pre-reading.

ADULT PREPARATION:

1. To create letter cards, use a broad-tipped marker to write alphabet letters. Write one letter on each index card. See Appendix C for samples of D'Nealian, Zanner Blouer, and Palmer writing styles. Check with your school as to the style of writing used.

2. Place letter cards in a basket on the table.

continued

1

Air Writing continued

ACTIVITY INTRODUCTION SUGGESTION:

"We are learning to write our alphabet letters. Today we will practice writing letters in the air. Your finger is your special air pen. The air is our invisible paper."

THEME INTRODUCTION SUGGESTION:

"Our unit is *transportation*. Some airplanes write messages in the sky. Today we're going to do air writing."

PROCEDURES:

The children will complete the following steps:

1. Lay the alphabet letter card flat on the table.
2. Identify the letter on the letter card.
3. Trace the alphabet letter with an index finger.
4. Hold the alphabet letter card upright.
5. With an index finger, write the letter in the air.
6. Repeat steps 1–5 with other letters.

VARIATION:

Write words or names on the letter cards.

BOOK SUGGESTION:

The Man Who Walked Between the Towers by Mordicai Gerstein (Brookfield, CT: Roaring Brook Press, 2003). This book presents an account of the 1974 act of Philippe Petit walking through the air between the World Trade Center towers.

Alligator Alphabet Puzzle

SKILL EXPLANATION:

Print awareness is developed through both the recognition of alphabet letters and the understanding that print is read left to right.

ADULT PREPARATION:

1. Use a pencil or pen to copy alligator pattern on green construction paper.
2. Write the lowercase alphabet between the dotted lines. Write the letters in sequential order.
3. Cut out the alligator, then cut it apart on the dotted lines.
4. Place the alligator pieces in a resealable plastic bag.
5. Place lowercase alphabet strip on the table.

ACTIVITY INTRODUCTION SUGGESTION:

Show the children the alphabet strip and say, "These are the letters of the alphabet. Let's sing the alphabet song." After the song is sung say, "Alligator starts with *a*. What is the first letter of the alphabet? When we put these alphabet pieces in order, they will make an alligator."

THEME INTRODUCTION SUGGESTION:

"Our unit is (pond life) (China) (Zoo). Today we will talk about alligators. They are found in ponds, countries such as China, and in zoos. Some alligators are green or brown. What does an alligator look like?"

PROCEDURES:

The child will complete the following steps:

1. Take the alligator pieces out of the bag.
2. Place the head of the alligator on the left.
3. Look at the lowercase alphabet guide to identify the first letter, with adult assistance if needed.
4. Look for the piece with the letter *a*. Place it after the head.

continued

AGES: 3–6

GROUP SIZE:
2 children

DEVELOPMENTAL GOALS:
- ✄ To recognize alphabet letters
- ✄ To develop left-to-right progression

LEARNING OBJECTIVE:
Using alligator alphabet puzzle pieces, the child will identify letters as they sequence the alphabet from left to right.

MATERIALS:
Alligator pattern (Appendix A1)
Pencil or pen
Green construction paper
Marker
Adult scissors
Resealable bag (quart or gallon size)
Lowercase alphabet strip

Alligator Alphabet Puzzle continued

5. Look for the piece with the letter *b*. Place it after *a*.

6. Find and place all alligator pieces in sequential order. The tail will be placed last.

NOTES:

✂ When children are unfamiliar with the alphabet, the lowercase alphabet strip should be used as a guide until their skill level increases.

✂ Both upper- and lowercase letters may be placed on each alligator piece. If two separate puzzles are made for each case, color-code the alligators (e.g., make the uppercase alligator green and the lowercase alligator brown).

BOOK SUGGESTIONS:

✂ *The Lady with the Alligator Purse* by Mary Ann Hoberman (New York: Little, Brown & Co., 2003). This humorous book has a story to read, music to sing with the text, and games to play.

✂ *Alligators all Around* by Maurice Sendak (New York: HarperCollins, 1962). Alligators are personified in a simple alphabet format.

4

Alphabet Children

A

AGES: 3–6

GROUP SIZE:
2–4 children

DEVELOPMENTAL GOALS:
✄ To recognize alphabet letters
✄ To promote physical development

LEARNING OBJECTIVE:
Using alphabet cards, the children will use their bodies to form alphabet letters.

MATERIALS:
Permanent marker
Construction paper
Digital camera or camera and film
Rubber cement
Hole punch
Three 2" metal rings

SKILL EXPLANATION:

Using physical actions aids recall, thus helping children learn the alphabet, which is essential for reading.

ADULT PREPARATION:

1. Using a permanent marker, write alphabet letters on individual pieces of construction paper.

ACTIVITY INTRODUCTION SUGGESTION:

"We can make letters of the alphabet using our bodies. We will work together to make the letters."

THEME INTRODUCTION SUGGESTION:

"Our unit is *valentines*. We will spell out 'I love you' with our bodies."

continued

Alphabet Children continued

PROCEDURES:

The children will complete the following steps:

1. Lay on the floor to create alphabet letters. For example three children would be needed to make an uppercase *N*. Two children would lay parallel to each other. The third child would lay diagonal between the two, touching the head of the child on the left and the feet of the child on the right.
2. Lay still while an adult takes a picture of the letter the children have formed with their bodies.
3. Repeat steps 1–2 for all 26 letters of the alphabet, allowing all children to have a turn.

The adult will complete the following steps:

1. Develop all pictures and glue them on the individual pages, with the alphabet letters, using rubber cement.
2. Create a cover titled *Our Alphabet Children.*
3. Punch holes in the pages and place them in order.
4. Bind the pages with metal rings and place in the book center.

NOTES:

- ✂ A large area will need to be cleared for the children to lay and form their letters.
- ✂ When taking pictures, note what is in the background. The best pictures will not have distractions.
- ✂ Additional books may be made for each child to take one home.
- ✂ This activity may be done with one or two letters weekly, where the book would develop over the course of many months.

BOOK SUGGESTIONS:

- ✂ *A B C Animals: A Bedtime Story* by Darice Bailer (New York: Little Simon, 2005). The little animals go through their bedtime routine. The pages for each alphabet animal are cut in the shape of the uppercase letter.
- ✂ *ABC USA* by Martin Jarrie (New York: Sterling Publishing Co., Inc., 2005). The author/illustrator looks at items that are uniquely American in an alphabet format. A glossary of these terms is provided in the back of the book.

Ants Go Marching through the Alphabet

SKILL EXPLANATION:

Recognizing and matching alphabet letters are stages of print awareness. Children will be able to move forward from this step to the understanding of phonics.

ADULT PREPARATION:

1. Use a pencil or pen to copy and cut out ant patterns on red construction paper.
2. Write a lowercase letter on each ant using a permanent marker.
3. Write uppercase letters on the plastic tablecloth in random order, using the permanent marker.

ACTIVITY INTRODUCTION SUGGESTION:

"We are going on a picnic. What is written on our picnic tablecloth? Sometimes ants show up at a picnic. These ants try to find the alphabet letter on the tablecloth that will match the letter on their back."

THEME INTRODUCTION SUGGESTION:

"Our unit is (insects) (bugs) (picnics) (summer fun). These ants are going on a picnic. They need to sit on their alphabet letter."

PROCEDURES:

The child will complete the following steps:

1. Identify a letter on the tablecloth.
2. Look for the ant with the matching letter.
3. Place the ant on the matching letter on the tablecloth.
4. Repeat steps 1–3 until all ants and alphabet letters have been matched.

AGES: 3–6

GROUP SIZE:
2–4 children

DEVELOPMENTAL GOALS:
- ✄ To recognize alphabet letters
- ✄ To pair upper- and lowercase letters

LEARNING OBJECTIVE:
Using ant cutouts and tablecloth squares, the child will identify and match the upper- and lowercase letters together.

MATERIALS:
Ant pattern
  (Appendix A2)
Pencil or pen
Red construction paper
Adult scissors
Permanent marker
Plastic tablecloth

continued

Ants Go Marching through the Alphabet continued

NOTE:

This activity may be done on the table or floor.

VARIATION:

For younger children, use only lowercase letters on the ants and tablecloth. Cut the tablecloth into smaller sections and limit the number of alphabet letters to identify on each section.

BOOK SUGGESTIONS:

- ✄ *One Hundred Hungry Ants* by Elinor J. Pinczes (Boston, MA: Houghton Mifflin Company). Ants miss out on the food at a picnic when they keep scrambling into rows. Children will enjoy helping say the repetitive phrases in this book.

- ✄ *I Saw an Ant on the Railroad Track* by Joshua Prince (New York: Sterling Publishing Co., Inc., 2006). Switchman Jack works to save an ant on the railroad track; he manages this when he shares his snack. The rhyming text and illustrations will delight children.

Bear Bag Story

AGES: 4–6

GROUP SIZE:
4–20 children

DEVELOPMENTAL GOALS:

✂ To develop listening skills

✂ To build recall and oral expression

LEARNING OBJECTIVE:

Using a bag, bears, bowls, toy chairs, wooden blocks, spoons, and a doll, the children will retell the story of *The Three Bears*.

MATERIALS:

Large paper grocery bag or shopping bag

Three stuffed toy bears (large, medium, and small)

Three bowls (large, medium, and small)

Three small toy chairs (large, medium, and small)

Three wooden blocks (large, medium, and small)

Doll with hair

Three spoons

SKILL EXPLANATION:

Children develop an appreciation of literacy by having others read to them. When others read to children, the children are able to develop listening skills, build vocabulary, and develop oral expression.

ADULT PREPARATION:

1. Put three sizes (large, medium, and small) of each of the following items in a large paper grocery bag or shopping bag:
   a. Stuffed toy bears
   b. Bowls
   c. Small toy chairs
   d. Wooden blocks to represent beds
2. Put a doll and three spoons in the bag.

continued

Bear Bag Story continued

ACTIVITY INTRODUCTION SUGGESTION:

"Today we are going to listen to a story about the three bears. This is a different type of story. We're going to tell this story from the things we have in our bag. Let's see what we have. Are they all the same size?"

THEME INTRODUCTION SUGGESTION:

"Our unit is (fairy tales) (bears). We are going to have a special story. This is a fairy tale about three bears. Our story isn't going to be told from a book today. Our story will come out of a bag."

PROCEDURES:

The children will watch the adult complete the following steps:

1. Pull the three bears out of the bag and say, "Once there were three bears, Papa Bear, Mama Bear, and Baby Bear."

2. Line the bears up in sequential order from largest to smallest.

3. Take the three bowls and spoons out of the bag.

4. Give the bowls to the bears in the following order:

   a. Large bowl to large bear

   b. Medium bowl to medium bear

   c. Small bowl to small bear

5. Place a spoon in each bowl and say, "The bears tasted their porridge and it was too hot, so they decided to go for a walk."

6. Put the bears back in the bag and pull the doll from the bag and say, "Goldilocks was walking through the woods and came to the bear's house. She opened the door and went inside."

7. Lift the spoon to the doll's mouth from the appropriate bowl when speaking.

   a. "When she saw the porridge on the table, she tasted from the largest bowl and said, 'This is too hot.'"

   b. "She took a taste from the medium-sized bowl and said, 'This is too cold.'"

   c. "She took a taste from the smallest bowl and said, 'This is just right.' And she ate it all."

8. Put the bowls back in the bag and remove the three chairs. Line them up from largest to smallest.

continued

Bear Bag Story continued

9. Set the doll in the appropriate sized chair as speaking:

   a. "Goldilocks sat in the largest chair and said, 'This is too hard.'"

   b. "Goldilocks sat in the middle-sized chair and said, 'This is too soft.'"

   c. "Goldilocks sat in the smallest chair and said, 'This is just right.'"

10. Tip the chair over and say, "But when she sat in the chair, she broke it."

11. Return the chairs to the bag and put out the blocks as beds, lining them up in sequential order from largest to smallest.

12. Place the doll in the appropriate bed when speaking.

    a. "Goldilocks was tired so she lay down on the largest bed and said, 'This bed is too hard.'"

    b. "Goldilocks lay on the medium-sized bed and said, 'This is too soft.'"

    c. "Goldilocks lay on the smallest bed and said, 'This is just right.' And she fell asleep.'"

13. Set the beds to the side. Pull the bowls and spoons out of the bag, and return them to their sequential order. Place the bears in front of their appropriate-sized bowl.

14. In a deep voice say, "Papa Bear said, 'Someone has been eating my porridge.'"

15. In a normal voice say, "Mama Bear said, 'Someone has been eating my porridge.'"

16. In a high voice say, "Baby Bear said, 'Someone has been eating my porridge and they ate it all!'"

17. Put the bowls and spoons back in the bag. Take the chairs out of the bag and place them in their sequential order with the smallest chair tipped on its side.

18. In a deep voice say, "Papa Bear said, 'Someone has been sitting in my chair.'"

19. In a normal voice say, "Mama Bear said, 'Someone has been sitting in my chair.'"

20. In a high voice say, "Baby Bear said, 'Someone has been sitting in my chair, and they broke it!'"

21. Put the chairs back in the bag and put the bed/blocks in their sequential order. The doll is on the smallest bed/block.

continued

Bear Bag Story continued

22. Place the bears in beside their appropriate-sized bed.

23. In a deep voice say, "Papa Bear said, 'Someone has been sleeping in my bed.'"

24. In a normal voice say, "Mama Bear said, 'Someone has been sleeping in my bed.'"

25. In a high voice say, "Baby Bear said, 'Someone has been sleeping in my bed and she's still here!'"

26. In a normal voice say, "The noise woke up Goldilocks. She jumped up, and when she saw the bears she ran away. The bears never saw Goldilocks again."

27. Put all items back in the bag.

The children will complete the following steps:

1. Take turns retelling the story of *Goldilocks and the Three Bears* using the bag and its props.

NOTE:

When the adult lines up the bears, bowls, chairs, and beds in sequential order from largest to smallest, place the item starting at the child's left. This ensures that as the items are discussed from largest to smallest, they are viewed in the left-to-right progression needed for reading.

VARIATION:

If these props are not available, use a different story for which props are readily accessible, such as *The Three Little Pigs* and *The Three Billy Goats Gruff.*

BOOK SUGGESTIONS:

✂ *Goldilocks and the Three Bears* by James Marshall (New York: Dial, 1988). Goldilocks doesn't like to do what she is told in this 1989 Caldecott Honor Book.

Book Buddies

SKILL EXPLANATION:

Children look up to older children. An appreciation of literacy will be developed when they see others reading and have older children read to them.

ADULT PREPARATION:

1. Invite an older group of children to join the younger children as *book buddies.* This may be an older class in an elementary school or school-aged children in a child care center.
2. Pair one reader to one non-reader.
3. Plan a time and place for all the book buddies to meet.

ACTIVITY INTRODUCTION SUGGESTION:

"Today we will have visitors from Mr. _____'s class. They are coming to read books with us. Each one of you will be paired with a buddy from Mr. _____'s class. They will be your *book buddy.*"

THEME INTRODUCTION SUGGESTION:

"Our unit is *friends.* Who is your friend? Today we are going to make a new friend. This friend will come from another class. They will be coming to our room once a week and will read a book with you. They are called a *book buddy.*"

PROCEDURES:

The child will complete the following steps:

1. Select a book.
2. Give the book to his or her book buddy.
3. Find a quiet place to sit together.
4. Listen to the book as the older child reads.

NOTES:

✄ The adult may provide a selection of books they would like read, matching a certain unit or theme. The child may also bring a book from home. If available, the child may visit the library to select a book.

✄ Children aged 4 and 5 prefer to be paired with the same gender for their book buddy.

continued

AGES: 4–6

GROUP SIZE:

1 younger child to 1 older child

DEVELOPMENTAL GOALS:

✄ To develop listening skills

✄ To promote social development

LEARNING OBJECTIVE:

With an older child and books, the child will listen as a story is read.

MATERIALS:

A selection of books (at least one book for each child)

Book Buddies continued

BOOK SUGGESTIONS:

✄ *Will I Have a Friend?* by Miriam Cohen (New York: Scholastic, Inc., 1967). Jim goes to his first day of school worried whether or not he would have a friend there.

✄ *Hey Al!* by Arthur Yorinks, illustrated by Richard Egielski. (New York: Farrar, Straus and Giroux, 1986). In this Caldecott Medal winner, a toucan leads a janitor and his dog to paradise, where they turn into birds. Gratefully, they find their way home and appreciate the life they have.

Building Sentences with Friends

SKILL EXPLANATION:

Fluency and comprehension are the later skills of reading. Both are developed as children continually practice to identify words and read sentences.

ADULT PREPARATION:

1. Use the ruler and pencil or pen; mark the tag board into 4″ × 12″ rectangles.

2. Use the scissors to cut the tag board into 4″ × 12″ pieces.

3. Make a set of word cards for each child by writing simple nouns and verbs on the tag board pieces with a permanent marker. Select words from Appendix B1.

continued

B

AGES: 4–6

GROUP SIZE:
6–16 children

DEVELOPMENTAL GOALS:

✂ To identify sight words

✂ To understand that sentences are made of words

LEARNING OBJECTIVE:

Using word necklaces, the children will build simple sentences.

MATERIALS:

Ruler
Pencil or pen
Adult scissors
Tag board
Dolch words
   (Appendix B1)
Permanent marker
Resealable bags
Hole punch
Yarn
Basket

Building Sentences with Friends continued

4. Place one set of these word cards in a resealable plastic bag for each child to take home.

5. Make a duplicate set of word cards and punch a hole in the top corners of this set.

6. Tie a length of yarn to each card creating a word necklace.

7. Place the word necklaces in a basket.

ACTIVITY INTRODUCTION SUGGESTION:

"We are going to use word necklaces to make sentences. Take a necklace out of the basket. Read the word and put the necklace on; make sure your word faces outward. Find someone whose word will make a sentence with your word."

THEME INTRODUCTION SUGGESTION:

"Our unit is *friends*. Each person will take a word out of the basket. Then you will find a friend. Put your words together to see if they make a sentence. If they don't make a sentence, find another friend; put your words together to see if they make a sentence.

PROCEDURES:

The children will complete the following steps:

1. Sit in a circle or semicircle.

2. Take turns pulling a word necklace out of the basket and identifying the word.

3. Say the word as a group.

4. Repeat steps 2 and 3 until all children have a word necklace.

5. Put the necklace on so the word lays visible on each person's chest.

6. Find another child with whom their word will make a sentence (e.g., Boy runs.).

NOTE:

Children's names may be used for the nouns.

continued

Building Sentences with Friends continued

VARIATIONS:

✂ To save on some adult preparation, children may just hold the words in front of them.

✂ If appropriate, pictures may be added to the word cards.

EXPANSIONS:

✂ If the sentence involves an action verb, have children act it out (e.g., Boy runs.).

✂ Give each child a resealable plastic bag of words so the child may continue to identify words and make sentences at home. Send home a family letter explaining what to do with the word cards (Appendix B2).

BOOK SUGGESTIONS:

✂ *Friends* by Rob Lewis (New York: Henry Holt & Co., 1999). Oscar learns how to make friends.

✂ *A Friend Like Ed* by Karen Wagner (New York: Scholastic, Inc., 1998). Mildred and Ed have been friends a long time. Their friendship is jeopardized, but it survives in the end.

Class Books

GROUP SIZE:
1–4

DEVELOPMENTAL GOALS:
- ✂ To develop oral language skills
- ✂ To associate words with corresponding print

LEARNING OBJECTIVE:
Using construction paper and markers, the children will dictate and draw a page for the class book.

MATERIALS:
9" × 12" construction paper
Washable markers
Hole punch
Three 2" metal rings
Laminator or clear contact paper

SKILL EXPLANATION:

An appreciation and desire for literacy is developed as children see the words they speak dictated into print.

ADULT PREPARATION:

1. Select a common theme such as families.
2. Be familiar with the names of the people the child lives with. This may be obtained from the child's application or by asking parents to send in a list of family members. This information will be used to write the child's family members' names correctly in step 4 of the child's procedures.
3. Fold a piece of 9" × 12" construction paper in half for each child, making it 9" × 6".
4. Write *Our Families* on a separate piece of 9" × 12" construction paper. This will be the cover page.

ACTIVITY INTRODUCTION SUGGESTION:

"Today we are going to talk about families. What are some of the names of people in your family? You will take turns telling me something about your family and then draw a picture of them. We are going to put all our stories together in a book to read and share with our families."

THEME INTRODUCTION SUGGESTION:

"Our unit is *family*. We are going to make a book about our families. Everyone will get a turn to tell me about their family, and I'll write it down; you will add a picture of your family by drawing it, then we will bind the pages together into a class family book."

PROCEDURES:

The children will complete the following steps:

1. Select a piece of folded construction paper.
2. Open the paper to lay flat.
3. Draw a picture of their family on the top half of the construction paper.

continued

18

Class Books continued

4. Individually dictate a story about his or her family while the adult writes it down on the bottom half of the paper. The adult may give the child story prompts such as "Our family likes to . . ."

The adult will complete the following steps:

1. Laminate each page, or cover the pages with clear contact paper.

2. Laminate the cover page and a blank sheet of construction paper for the back of the book. If a laminator is not available, cover these pages with clear contact paper.

3. Align and punch three holes in each page.

4. Make a class book by binding all the children's pages together with metal rings through the holes.

5. Read the book to the children.

NOTE:

Depending upon the age group, ability, or attention span, children may dictate a sentence or two rather than a story.

VARIATION:

Title the book *Whose Family is This?* Start each page with the title, then have the child dictate about their family. When reading, the children may guess whose family it is. When the page is turned, the child will be identified by their name on the back of their page.

NOTE:

Other common themes to select are pets, pets they'd like to have, or how a holiday is celebrated. Story starters may also be used, examples are:

✄ A fun one would be "If I woke up and found a dinosaur in my backyard, I'd . . ."

✄ "If I gave a mouse a _____, he'd . . . ."

✄ "When I grow up, it would be exciting to . . . ."

EXPANSION:

Allow the children to have turns taking the book home to read with their families.

continued

Class Books continued

BOOK SUGGESTIONS:

- ✂ *If You Give a Mouse A Cookie* by Laurie Joffe (New York: Harper & Row, 1985). Giving a mouse a cookie starts a chain of events.
- ✂ *If the Dinosaurs Came Back* by Bernard Most. (San Diego: Harcourt, Inc., 1978). The dinosaurs would be very useful to people if they were alive today.

Classmate Bingo

AGES: 3–6

GROUP SIZE:
6–18 children

DEVELOPMENTAL GOALS:
- ✂ To develop word recognition
- ✂ To promote visual discrimination

LEARNING OBJECTIVE:
Using a picture sheet and counters, the children will match classmates' names to their pictures.

MATERIALS:
Permission form to be photographed and videotaped (Appendix B3)
Digital camera or camera and film
Pictures of children
Adult scissors
Card stock paper
Rubber cement
Index cards
Permanent marker
Counters (large buttons or milk caps)
Basket

SKILL EXPLANATION:

Fluency is developed as children recognize familiar words such as names. Young children have a tendency to first match only the initial letter. Visual discrimination aids this process as they look beyond the initial letter to match the letters of their classmates' names.

ADULT PREPARATION:

1. Make sure there is a copy of the permission form on file for each child to be photographed (Appendix B3).
2. Take and develop a picture of each child.
3. Copy the pictures and cut them into 2″ × 3″ rectangles.
4. Glue 6 to 9 pictures on a sheet of card stock paper. Write each child's name under their picture. Make one picture sheet for each child. The pictures of the children on the sheets may vary.
5. Write the children's names on individual index cards.
6. Gather large buttons or milk caps to use as counters. Put the counters in a basket.

continued

Classmate Bingo continued

ACTIVITY INTRODUCTION SUGGESTION:

"We are going to play bingo. On our bingo cards we have pictures of our school friends. When I say a person's name, see if their picture is on your card. If their picture is on your card, place a marker on their picture."

THEME INTRODUCTION SUGGESTION:

"Our unit is (friends) (my school). We have friends at school. What is the name of our school? What are the names of the people in your class? Pictures of your friends at school are on these cards."

PROCEDURES:

The children will complete the following steps:

1. Select a picture sheet and 6–9 counters.
2. Watch the adult hold up an index card with a classmate's name.
3. Identify the name on the card.
4. Look for the name and child's picture on their picture sheet.
5. If their picture sheet has that child's picture, place a counter on the child's picture.
6. Repeat steps 2–5 until all children have had their name shown and picture covered with a counter.

⚠ SAFETY PRECAUTION:

Use large counters with young children to prevent choking. Test items in a choke tube or toilet roll. A choke tube is a small-parts tester. If an item fits into the choke tube or toilet roll, it is considered to be a potential choking hazard. Choke tubes may be purchased at toy or baby stores.

BOOK SUGGESTION:

Miss Bindergarten Gets Ready for Kindergarten by Joseph Slate (New York: Scholastic, Inc., 1996). Animals are personified as they get ready for Miss Bindergarten's class. The animal classmates are presented in alphabetical order. Each letter of the alphabet is represented.

Clothesline Story

GROUP SIZE:
2–4 children

DEVELOPMENTAL GOALS:
- ✂ To develop listening skills
- ✂ To enhance visual discrimination

LEARNING OBJECTIVE:
Using comics, yarn, and snap clothespins, the children will retell a story.

MATERIALS:
Adult scissors
Duplicate comics from newspaper
Laminator or clear contact paper
Yarn
Tape measure or yardstick
Two baskets
Snap clothespins

SKILL EXPLANATION:

An appreciation of literacy is developed as the comic is read to children. They will develop this stage of reading as they listen to the story in order to retell it. Visual discrimination helps the child tell the sequence of action from the pictures.

ADULT PREPARATION:

1. Cut two sets of duplicate comics from the newspaper. Choose comics that are age-appropriate.
2. Laminate the comics or cover them in clear contact paper.
3. Cut one comic into sections.
4. String a length of yarn measuring 4' in a section of the room.
5. Place the cutout comic sections in a basket.
6. Place snap clothespins in a second basket.

ACTIVITY INTRODUCTION SUGGESTION:

"Today we are going to listen to a story from comics. These comics are picture stories found in the newspaper. After listening to the story, we are going to take pieces of the story out of a basket and then put them in order. We'll put them in order of what happened first, what happened second, and so on. Instead of just laying the story pieces on the table, we will hang them on a clothesline."

continued

Clothesline Story continued

PROCEDURES:

The children will complete the following steps:

1. Listen to the adult read the comic that has not been cut apart. Look at the pictures as the adult reads.

2. Take turns selecting sections of the comic from the basket and clipping them on the yarn in the order of the story.

3. Once all sections are clipped in place, retell the story.

BOOK SUGGESTION:

Jesse Bear, What Will You Wear? By Nancy White Carlstrom (New York: Simon & Schuster, 1986). Jesse Bear's day is chronicled in rhyme.

Collage

AGES: 3–6

GROUP SIZE:
2–4 children

DEVELOPMENTAL GOALS:
- ✂ To identify beginning sounds
- ✂ To develop listening skills

LEARNING OBJECTIVE:
Using construction paper, magazines, scissors, and glue, the child will make a collage.

MATERIALS:
Permanent marker
Construction paper
Magazines, newspapers, or advertisements
Adult scissors
White school glue

SKILL EXPLANATION:

The ability to identify an alphabet letter and associate it with its sound is phonics. As children sound out the name of pictures and emphasize the first sound in the picture, phonemic awareness is developed.

ADULT PREPARATION:

1. To focus on a specific alphabet letter, write the upper- and lowercase letter at the top of a sheet of construction paper, using a permanent marker. Make one for each child, using the same letter on each sheet.
2. Write children's names at the bottom of the individual sheets of construction paper.
3. Cut pictures out of magazines, newspapers, or advertisements that began with that letter.

ACTIVITY INTRODUCTION SUGGESTION:

"Today we are making a collage. A collage is a lot of pictures glued together. I'm going to show you some pictures I've cut. Say the name of these pictures. All the pictures start with the same sound. All the pictures start with the letter _____. Now you can choose as many pictures as you like to glue together to make your own collage."

continued

Collage continued

THEME INTRODUCTION SUGGESTION:

"Our unit is *art*. What does an artist do? Some artists work with paint or sculptures. Some artists make a collage. We will make a collage by gluing pictures on a paper. All the items on our collage will start with the letter _____."

PROCEDURES:

The child will complete the following steps:

1. Take the sheet of construction paper with their name.
2. Identify the letter on the top of the construction paper.
3. Make the sound of that letter. If the child has difficulty, listen to the adult make that letter sound.
4. Select and identify pictures already cut.
5. Emphasize the beginning sound in each picture by repeating the picture word and then saying its beginning sound.
6. Glue the pictures on their sheet of construction paper.

NOTE:

Older children may look through the magazines, newspapers, or advertisements; they may cut their own pictures.

VARIATIONS:

✄ Cut the paper in the shape of the letter.

✄ Display the finished pages on the walls around the room for additional reinforcement.

BOOK SUGGESTION:

The legend of the Indian Paintbrush by Tomie DePaola (New York: Putnam, 1988). Little Gopher follows his dream and becomes an artist. He seeks the colors of the sunset and finally finds them on brushes all around him on the ground. The next morning, the brushes have taken root and blossomed into flowers.

Color Words

SKILL EXPLANATION:

Fluency is developed as a child practices reading color words. By being able to match the color word to the specific crayon, the child is able to demonstrate comprehension.

ADULT PREPARATION:

1. Write color words on individual index cards, using lowercase letters.
2. Select crayons of the same colors.
3. Place the crayons in a basket.

ACTIVITY INTRODUCTION SUGGESTION:

"Today we are going to talk about colors. What color is the sun? What color is the sky? We are going to match crayons to the word that says the same color." Show the children a crayon and ask, "What color is this? Show me the card with the same color word. Now we will match the rest of the crayons to their color words."

PROCEDURES:

The child will complete the following steps:

1. Lay the index cards in a row on the table.
2. Identify the color words from left to right.
3. Identify the color of each crayon and place the crayon on the matching color word.
4. Repeat step 3 until all crayons and words are matched.

NOTE:

Color words may be written in the specific color for younger children (i.e., write the word "blue" with a blue marker).

BOOK SUGGESTIONS:

✄ *Take a Walk on a Rainbow: A First Look at Color* by Miriam Moss (Minneapolis, MN: Picture Window Books, 1999). A girl and her grandfather explore the colors around them.

C

continued

Color Words continued

- *Colors* by Alvin Granowsky (Brookfield, CT: Copper Beech Books, 2001). Jo's clothes are colorful and match the colors of many other things.

- *Brown Bear, Brown Bear, What Do You See?* by Bill Martin, Jr. (New York: Henry Holt & Co., 1967). This children's classic starts with what Brown Bear sees, ending with what a class of children see.

Dandy Dictionary

SKILL EXPLANATION:

An appreciation of literacy is shown through vocabulary development. Fluency is developed through the identification of words.

ADULT PREPARATION:

1. Use the three-hole punch to make holes in copy paper, one for each letter of the alphabet. Twenty-six pages will be needed for each child.

ACTIVITY INTRODUCTION SUGGESTION:

"A dictionary is a special book with lots of words. A dictionary tells us what each word means. Today we are going to start page 1 of your own dictionary. Each day we will glue a picture and write the word under the picture."

THEME INTRODUCTION SUGGESTION:

"Our unit is *books*. A dictionary is a special book. We will make a picture dictionary by gluing one picture on each page and writing the word under the picture."

PROCEDURES:

The child will complete the following steps:

1. Cut pictures from a magazine.
2. Lay the paper with the holes punched on the left.
3. Glue one picture at the top of each page.
4. Identify the picture.
5. Watch the adult use the fine-tipped marker to lightly write the word under the picture by creating a series of dots to form the word.
6. Use a pencil to trace the dots to create the word.
7. Allow the glue to dry.

The adult will complete the following steps:

1. Alphabetize each child's pages.
2. Place each child's pages in individual three-prong folders.
3. Place a label on the outside of the folder.
4. Write the possessive form of the child's name on the folder with the word *dictionary* (e.g., Karen's Dictionary).

continued

AGES: 4–6

GROUP SIZE:

2–5 children

DEVELOPMENTAL GOALS:

- ✂ To encourage vocabulary development
- ✂ To identify words

LEARNING OBJECTIVE:

Using a three-prong folder, magazines, child-size safety scissors, copy paper, glue, and a pencil or fine-tipped marker, the child will make their own picture dictionary.

MATERIALS:

Three-hole punch
Copy paper
Child-size safety scissors
Magazines
White school glue
Fine-tipped marker
Pencil
Three-prong folder

D

Dandy Dictionary continued

NOTE:

Children may decorate their folders.

BOOK SUGGESTIONS:

The following books are examples of dictionaries to share with children.

✀ *Simms Taback's Big Book of Words* by Simms Taback (Maplewood, NJ: Blue Apple Books). Single words are illustrated by Caldecott Medalist Simms Taback.

✀ *Picture Dictionary* by the editors of the American Heritage Dictionaries (New York: Houghton Mifflin Company, 2007). Each page is divided into four or five blocks. Each block has a single word, a sentence using that word, and an illustration.

Do You Hear What I Hear?

AGES: 3–6

GROUP SIZE:
4–20 children

DEVELOPMENTAL GOALS:
- ✂ To develop auditory discrimination
- ✂ To develop print awareness

LEARNING OBJECTIVE:
Using a blank audio tape and tape recorder, the children will identify familiar sounds.

MATERIALS:
Tape recorder
Blank audio tape
Permanent marker
Chart tablet or large paper

SKILL EXPLANATION:
An appreciation of literacy and print awareness is developed as the children practice auditory discrimination listening to sounds, then seeing the sound associated with the written word.

ADULT PREPARATION:
1. Tape record familiar sounds (e.g., running water, door shutting, dog barking, telephone ringing, bells ringing, etc.).

ACTIVITY INTRODUCTION SUGGESTION:
"What part of your body helps you hear? Today we will use our ears to listen to a sound. We'll take turns saying what the sound could be. I'll write what you say on the paper."

THEME INTRODUCTION SUGGESTION:
"Our unit is *the five senses*. We use our eyes to see, our nose to smell, our hands to touch, and our tongue to taste. Another one of our senses is hearing. What part of your body helps you hear? We will use our ears to listen to sounds. After we hear the sound, we will take turns saying what could make the sound. I'll write your guesses on this piece of paper."

continued

Do You Hear What I Hear? continued

PROCEDURES:

The children will complete the following steps:

1. Listen to adult play one sound at a time.
2. Take turns identifying the sound.
3. Watch the adult write the identified sound on a chart tablet or large sheet of paper.
4. Repeat steps 1–3 until all sounds are heard and identified.
5. Rewind the tape and listen to the sounds one by one.

The adult will complete the following steps:

1. The adult will stop the tape after each sound and read the words associated with the sound.
2. If the sound was not correctly identified, the adult will identify the sound.

BOOK SUGGESTION:

Lentil by Robert McCloskey. (New York: The Viking Press, 1940). Lentil saves the day with his harmonica in this classic tale.

Doggie, Doggie, Where's Your Bone?

SKILL EXPLANATION:

The children will develop an appreciation of literature and print awareness as they say the chant and follow the words and pictures in a left-to-right progression.

ADULT PREPARATION:

1. Enlarge the *Doggie, Doggie, Where's Your Bone* Rebus Chant (Appendix D1) and *Doggie, Doggie, Where's Your Bone* Rebus Recipe (Appendix D2).
2. Place flour in a large bowl.
3. Pour beef broth in a second bowl.
4. Set ½ cup measure beside the flour on the table.
5. Set the ⅛ cup measure beside the broth on the table.
6. Cover baking sheet with aluminum foil.
7. Set a chair in the group time area.
8. Place a wooden block under the chair to represent a bone.

continued

AGES: 4–6

GROUP SIZE:
6–12 children

DEVELOPMENTAL GOALS:
✄ To develop oral language
✄ To develop left-to-right progression

LEARNING OBJECTIVE:
Using rebus charts, the children will chant and then make dog biscuits.

MATERIALS:
Copy paper
Doggie, Doggie, Where's Your Bone rebus chant (Appendix D1)
Doggie, Doggie, Where's Your Bone rebus recipe (Appendix D2)
Flour
Large bowl
15 oz. can beef broth
Nesting measuring cups (½ cup & ⅛ cup)
Baking sheet
Aluminum foil
Chair
Wooden block
Bowls
Spoons
Permanent marker
Resealable plastic bags

D

Doggie, Doggie, Where's Your Bone? continued

ACTIVITY INTRODUCTION SUGGESTION:

"What do dogs eat for a treat? Today we will play *Doggie, Doggie, Where's Your Bone?* We'll use this wooden block for a bone. Then we will make a real dog treat, a dog biscuit, you can give to a dog you know."

THEME INTRODUCTION SUGGESTION:

"Our unit is *pets*. Today we will play *Doggie, Doggie, Where's Your Bone?* Then we will make a dog biscuit you can take to a dog you know."

PROCEDURES:

The children will complete the following steps:

1. Sit in a semicircle on the floor.
2. Look at the rebus chart and say the chant together.
3. Take turns being the dog and sitting in the chair with his or her back towards the semicircle.
4. The child in the "dog chair" will close their eyes. They may cover them with their hands.
5. One child will be selected to sneak up the chair and remove the "bone."
6. The children sitting in the semicircle will read the rebus chart and chant, "Doggie, doggie, where's your bone, someone took it from your home."
7. The child in the "dog chair" will turn around and get three guesses to determine who took the "bone."
8. Once the child has guessed three times the person holding the "bone" will replace it under the chair and may have the opportunity to play the dog.
9. Repeat steps 4–8 until all children have had a chance to be the dog.
10. Wash hands.
11. Take turns to look at the rebus recipe.
12. Scoop ½ cup flour into a bowl.
13. Scoop ⅛ cup of beef broth into the same bowl.

continued

34

Doggie, Doggie, Where's Your Bone? continued

14. Stir until a dough consistency is achieved. Add more broth if the dough is too dry to mold. Add more flour if the dough is too sticky to mold.

15. Mold the dough into a dog biscuit.

16. Place the biscuit on a foil-covered baking sheet.

17. Write name on the foil under their biscuit, with adult assistance if needed.

The adult will complete the following steps:

1. Preheat oven to 400°.

2. Once the baking sheet is full, place it in the oven for 30 minutes or until golden brown.

3. Allow the biscuits to cool and then put them in resealable plastic bags for the children to take home.

NOTES:

✂ Baking times will vary depending upon the thickness of the dough.

✂ ⅛ cup = 2 tablespoons

Egg Word Creations

GROUP SIZE:

2–4 children

DEVELOPMENTAL GOALS:

✂ To identify beginning and ending sounds

✂ To identify alphabet letters

LEARNING OBJECTIVE:

Using plastic eggs, the child will identify beginning and ending sounds to create words.

MATERIALS:

Plastic eggs
Permanent marker
Two baskets

SKILL EXPLANATION:

When a child identifies phonemes (sounds) and graphemes (letters that represent those sounds), they are demonstrating an understanding of phonics.

ADULT PREPARATION:

1. Using a permanent marker, write a beginning consonant on the smaller half of each egg. Use the letters *m*, *b*, and *s*.

2. Write the letters *et*, *at*, and *it* on the other egg halves.

3. Put the small halves with one letter in one basket.

4. Put the large halves with two letters in another basket.

continued

Egg Word Creations continued

ACTIVITY INTRODUCTION SUGGESTION:

"We are going to make words by putting together two halves of the eggs. These eggs have the letters *m, b,* or *s* on them. What sound does *m* make? What sound does *b* make? What sound does *s* make? The other egg halves have *et* (|et|), *at* (|at|), and *it* (|it|) on them. Choose a half, tell me the sound. Choose another half, tell me the sound. Put the two halves together; say the sounds together; then you've said a word."

THEME INTRODUCTION SUGGESTION:

Hold up egg and ask, "What are some animals that lay eggs? This week's unit is (Easter) (farm) (birds). (Chickens live on a farm.) (We dye chicken eggs at Easter time). Other birds also lay eggs. The chickens and birds sit on their eggs, keeping them warm until the baby chick or bird hatches. We are going to make words today by putting together two halves of the eggs."

PROCEDURES:

The child will complete the following steps:

1. Take a small egg half from the first basket; identify the letter and the letter sound.
2. Take a large egg half from the second basket; identify the letters and the ending sound.
3. Snap the egg halves together.
4. Joining the beginning and ending sounds, say the word.

NOTE:

For younger children, write an uppercase alphabet letter on one half and the corresponding lowercase alphabet letter on the other half. Have children identify and match alphabet letters.

BOOK SUGGESTION:

The Egg Tree by Katherine Milhous (New York: Atheneum Books for Young Readers, 1950). Children dye and paint eggs for their egg tree. This classic received the Caldecott Medal in 1951 and has inspired children across the country to make their own egg trees.

E

Endless Ending Sounds

AGES: 3–6

GROUP SIZE:

2–4 children

DEVELOPMENTAL GOALS:

✄ To identify ending sounds

✄ To develop auditory discrimination

LEARNING OBJECTIVE:

Using shoe boxes, index cards, a toy car, star, plastic jar, moon, spoon, pot, knot, dot, cat, hat, and mat, the child will identify ending sounds.

MATERIALS:

Index cards
Permanent marker
Masking tape
Shoe boxes (4)
Basket
Toy car
Toy star
Plastic jar
Toy moon
Spoon
Pot
Knot
Dot
Cat
Hat
Mat

SKILL EXPLANATION:

Phonemic awareness is developed through hearing and identifying sounds in rhyming objects. The understanding of phonics is used as children identify the sounds in letter blends.

ADULT PREPARATION:

1. Write the following ending sounds on index cards with a permanent marker: *ar, oon, ot,* and *at.*

2. Tape the index cards to individual shoe boxes.

3. Put the following small items in a basket: toy car, star, plastic jar, moon, spoon, pot, knot, dot, cat, hat, and mat.

ACTIVITY INTRODUCTION SUGGESTION:

"Today we are talking about rhyming. Rhyming is when different words sound almost the same. They have the same ending sounds like cat, hat, and mat." Show each of the items and with the children say the name of each item out loud. Now show the index cards with the ending sounds. "Ending sounds are the sounds you hear at the end of a word like the |at| in hat and cat. Now you will choose an item, say the word, find the ending sound, and place it in the box with that sound."

THEME INTRODUCTION SUGGESTION:

"Our unit is (rhyming) (Dr. Seuss). Rhyming is when different words sound almost the same, like cat, hat, and mat. They all have the same ending sound. Look at the items on the table. Say the names of the items. What is their ending sound? Find the box whose letters make the same ending sound. Put the item in that box."

PROCEDURES:

The child will complete the following steps:

1. With adult help if necessary, say the ending sounds on the cards attached to the shoe boxes.

continued

38

Endless Ending Sounds continued

2. Select and identify an item from the basket.

3. Identify the ending sound of the item and place it in the shoe box with those letters.

BOOK SUGGESTIONS:

✂ *Green Eggs and Ham* by Dr. Seuss (New York: Random House, 1960). Sam convinces his friend to try green eggs and ham in this rhyming text.

✂ *How Do You Say It Today, Jesse Bear?* by Nancy White Carlstrom (New York: Scholastic, Inc., 1992). Jesse Bear has a message with a rhyme for every month of the year.

Everlasting Puffy Paint Words

AGES: 4–6

GROUP SIZE:

2–4 children

DEVELOPMENTAL GOALS:

- ✂ To identify sight words
- ✂ To practice writing skills

LEARNING OBJECTIVE:

Using an index card, smock, and puffy paint, the child will identify and trace a word.

MATERIALS:

Bowl
Flour
Salt
Water
Liquid watercolor or food coloring
Spoon
Small squeeze bottles
Pencil
Index cards
Permanent marker
Dolch words (Appendix B1)
Baskets
Smock

SKILL EXPLANATION:

Fluency is developed through the practice of identifying sight words. Writing the word helps reinforce the identification.

ADULT PREPARATION:

1. In a bowl, mix equal portions of the following ingredients together with a spoon to make puffy paint:

   a. Flour

   b. Salt

   c. Water tinted with liquid watercolor or food coloring

2. Put the puffy paint into small squeeze bottles.

3. Write sight words on plain index cards with a marker. Select sight words from Appendix B1.

4. Place sight words in a basket. Place plain index cards in a separate basket.

continued

Everlasting Puffy Paint Words continued

ACTIVITY INTRODUCTION SUGGESTION:

"Today we are going to make words with a special paint. Puffy paint gets bigger after it dries. This paint puffs out. After it dries, we can feel the letters with our fingers."

THEME INTRODUCTION SUGGESTION:

"Our unit is (cooking) (baking). Who makes cakes? A chef may bake cakes. After they are baked, the cakes might be decorated. Sometimes we write words on cakes. What words are written on a birthday cake? Today we will make puffy paint words. When they dry, the letters are puffy and fun to feel."

PROCEDURES:

The child will complete the following steps:

1. Put on a smock.
2. Select and identify a sight word written on an index card.
3. Take a plain index card and copy the sight word onto the card with a pencil.
4. Use the small squeeze bottle of puffy paint and trace over the letters and let them dry.
5. Repeat steps 2–4 with other word cards.
6. Once the cards are dry, trace over the raised letters with a finger as each word is spelled.

VARIATIONS:

✂ For younger children, step 3 may be eliminated, and have the children trace on the prewritten cards with the puffy paint.

✂ Rather than words, alphabet letters may be used for younger children who need practice identifying or writing letters.

BOOK SUGGESTION:

Benny Bakes a Cake by Eve Rice. (New York: Greenwillow Books, 1981). Benny helps bake his cake on his birthday only to have his dog, Ralph, eat it. However, his dad and sister save the day.

Family Book

AGES: 3–6

GROUP SIZE:

2–4 children

DEVELOPMENTAL GOALS:

- ✂ To associate words with corresponding print
- ✂ To develop listening skills

LEARNING OBJECTIVE:

Using paper, crayons, markers, or colored pencils, the child will dictate statements about a parent or guardian.

MATERIALS:

Word processor (Optional)
Copy paper
Pen
18″ × 12″ construction paper
Permanent marker
Crayons, markers, or colored pencils
Stapler and staples

SKILL EXPLANATION:

The child will develop an appreciation of literacy as they listen to the adult read the sentence. The child will also develop print awareness as he or she dictates and watches spoken words being written.

ADULT PREPARATION:

1. Type or write sentences on a sheet of paper, leaving a blank for the child to respond.
2. Make one copy for each child.
3. The questions may include:

   a. My dad is _____ feet tall.

   b. My mom's first name is _____.

   c. My dad's favorite television show is _____.

   d. My mom's favorite food is _____.

   e. My dad's favorite game is _____.

   f. My mom likes to play _____.

4. To create a cover, fold a sheet of 18″ × 12″ construction paper in half.
5. Using a permanent marker write *My Parents* at the top of the front cover.
6. Write *By* on the bottom left of the front cover.

ACTIVITY INTRODUCTION SUGGESTION:

"We are going to make a book about our families. I will ask you some questions and then write down what you tell me. You will also draw a picture on the front cover. We will put your book together and you can share it with your family."

THEME INTRODUCTION SUGGESTION:

"Our unit is *families*. What are the names of some people in your family? Some families are really big and some are just two people. We all come from different families. We are going to make a book about our families."

continued

Family Book continued

PROCEDURES:

The child will complete the following steps:

1. Answer the questions, watching the adult writes down the answers to:

    a. How tall is your dad?

    b. What is your mom's first name?

    c. What is your dad's favorite television show?

    d. What is your mom's favorite food?

    e. What is your dad's favorite game?

    f. What does your mom like to play?

2. Draw on the front of the cover.

3. Write his or her name after the word *By*. If unable to write, the adult may assist or write the name.

The adult will complete the following steps:

1. Place the paper in the center fold of the cover.

2. Close the cover and staple the page inside the cover.

NOTE:

Be aware of the children's backgrounds. If a child doesn't have two parents, the sentence would be changed to reflect only the existing parent (i.e., Dad would be the subject of all statements). In other instances, the child may not live with either parent, and the subject would be changed to the primary caregiver.

VARIATION:

For a holiday unit on Thanksgiving, the book's name might be *Our Thanksgiving Dinner* and the following sentences may be used:

a. A turkey weighs _____.

b. A turkey cooks for _____ hours.

c. The oven needs to be _____ degrees.

d. The dinner takes _____ minutes to prepare.

continued

Family Book continued

BOOK SUGGESTIONS:

- ✂ *Hold my Hand: Five Stories of Love and Family* by Charlotte Zolotow (New York: Hyperion Books for Children, 2003). Five family stories are told. They are stories of a mother and baby boy, a big brother and little brother, a big brother and little sister, a father and little girl, and a poem illustrated with a man and child.

- ✂ *Weird Parents* by Audrey Wood (New York: Puffin Books, 1990). A boy has weird parents who embarrass him. He wishes they weren't weird, or that everyone had weird parents, but finally comes to terms that they are his parents.

- ✂ *I'll Always Be Your Friend* by Sam McBratney (HarperCollins Publishers, 2001). A little fox discovers his mother is his friend.

Finger Paint Writing

AGES: 4–6

GROUP SIZE:
4–6 children

DEVELOPMENTAL GOALS:
- ✂ To develop print awareness
- ✂ To enhance fine motor control

LEARNING OBJECTIVES:
Using finger paint, the children will write their names.

MATERIALS:
Permanent marker
Index cards
Newspaper
Trays
Smocks
Washable finger paint
Spoons
Construction paper (white)
Large mirror

SKILL EXPLANATION:

Fluency is enhanced as children recognize their names. Print awareness is developed by seeing their names in print and then writing them. Writing skills are developed through writing with another medium.

ADULT PREPARATION:

1. Write each child's name with a permanent marker on an individual index card.
2. Cover the table with newspaper. Set the trays, paints, and spoons on the table.

ACTIVITY INTRODUCTION SUGGESTION:

"How can you write your name backwards on paper? Today we will write our names on a tray and then transfer it to a sheet of paper, where it will look backwards."

THEME INTRODUCTION SUGGESTION:

"Our unit is *the five senses*. How does finger paint feel? Today we will write our names with finger paint."

continued

Finger Paint Writing continued

PROCEDURES:

The children will complete the following steps:

1. Find their name beside the tray.
2. Put on smocks.
3. Place a spoonful of finger paint on individual trays.
4. Rub the paint around the tray.
5. Using an index finger, write their name in the finger paint.
6. Set a piece of white construction paper on the tray.
7. Rub hands all over the paper.
8. Lift the paper and see the imprint of a name of the sheet. (Note the letters will be backwards from the letters on the tray.)
9. Set the paper on the counter or a rack to dry.
10. Once the paper is dry, hold it up to a mirror.
11. The letters that were backwards may be read correctly in the mirror.

Fishy Words

AGES: 5–7

GROUP SIZE:
2–4 children

DEVELOPMENTAL GOALS:

✄ To recognize high frequency words

✄ To coordinate muscles

LEARNING OBJECTIVE:

Using magnetic fish and a fishing pole, the child will recognize high frequency words.

MATERIALS:

Fish pattern (Appendix A3)
Construction paper
Adult scissors
Dolch word list (Appendix B1)
Marker
Paper clips (metal)
Magnetic wand
Heavyweight string
1'–3' pole
Large plastic tub
Small pail

SKILL EXPLANATION:

High frequency words are those used most often in spoken and written language (e.g., *The* is the word used most often.) The high frequency list is also known as the Dolch word list. These 220 words are listed in order of frequency. Children develop fluency as they learn to recognize these words. Pairing learning with a physical act (using the fishing pole to "catch" word cards) further aids the retention.

ADULT PREPARATION:

1. Copy and cut out fish patterns.
2. Select Dolch words and write one word on each fish.
3. Attach a metal paper clip to each fish.

continued

Fishy Words continued

4. To create a fishing pole, attach a magnetic wand to a 1'–3' pole with a 1'–2' length of heavyweight string.

5. Place the fish in a large plastic tub.

6. Place a small pail beside the large plastic tub.

ACTIVITY INTRODUCTION SUGGESTION:

"Today we are going fishing. Instead of catching regular fish, we are going to catch fishy words. When you catch a fishy word, tell me the name written on the fish. If you are right, you may put the fish in the small bucket. If you need to try again, you may put the fish back in the tub."

THEME INTRODUCTION SUGGESTION:

"Our unit is (ocean) (pond life) (water). What are some animals that live in the (ocean) (pond) (water)? Fish live in the (ocean) (pond) (water). Today we will catch a special fish. Today we will catch fishy words."

PROCEDURES:

The child will complete the following steps:

1. Use the fishing pole to "catch" a word fish.

2. Pull the fish out of the tub.

3. Identify the word on the fish.

4. If the word is correctly identified, place it in the small bucket.

5. If the word is incorrectly identified, listen to the adult say the correct word, and then place it back in the large plastic tub, to be caught again.

6. Repeat steps 1–5 until all fish have been caught and identified.

NOTES:

✄ Dolch words are high frequency words, and the first 100 words are given in order of frequency of use in the Appendix.

✄ Magnetic wands are found in teacher supply stores or catalogs. If the wand style of magnet is not available, a regular magnet may be used.

✄ Children will need practice with high frequency words before doing this activity.

continued

Fishy Words continued

BOOK SUGGESTIONS:

✁ *A Good Day's Fishing* by James Prosek (New York: Simon & Schuster, 2004). A boy searches through his tackle box remembering the fish he caught with different equipment. This book includes a fishing glossary.

✁ *I Love Fishing* by Bonnie Dobkin (Chicago: Children's Press, 1993). A little boy goes fishing. However, he watches bugs, makes mud pies, and does everything but fish. This easy reader has one simple sentence to accompany each picture page. The text is in rhyme.

Flexible Flannel Board Stories

AGES: 3–6

GROUP SIZE:

2–4 children

DEVELOPMENTAL GOALS:

✂ To develop listening skills

✂ To enhance oral expression

LEARNING OBJECTIVE:

Using a flannel board and flannel board pieces, the children will listen to and then retell a story.

MATERIALS:

Coloring book
Crayons or colored pencils
Adult scissors
Laminator or clear contact paper
Sandpaper or felt
Hot glue gun
Hot glue gun sticks

SKILL EXPLANATION:

An appreciation of literacy is developed as children listen to a story. This appreciation is enhanced through recall and retelling the story.

ADULT PREPARATION:

1. Select a coloring book that tells a story.
2. Color and cut out characters from the story.
3. Laminate the characters, or cover them with clear contact paper.
4. Cut strips of sandpaper or felt and hot glue them to the back of the laminated characters.

ACTIVITY INTRODUCTION SUGGESTION:

"What is a flannel board? It is a special board covered with flannel material to help things stick to it. What sticks to a flannel board? We will tell a story by moving pieces on the flannel board."

THEME INTRODUCTION SUGGESTION:

"Our unit is *nursery rhymes*. We will tell our nursery rhyme using a flannel board."

PROCEDURES:

The children will complete the following steps:

1. Listen as the adult tells the story.
2. Move the characters on, off, and around the flannel board as the story dictates.
3. Retell the story as they move the characters on the flannel board.

NOTE:

Children may create original stories with the flannel board pieces.

continued

Flexible Flannel Board Stories continued

BOOK SUGGESTIONS:

✄ For other flannel board stories use *The Complete Daily Curriculum* by Pam Schiller and Pat Phipps (Beltsville, MD: Gryphon House, 2002). This book contains flannel board stories and nearly 50 pages of flannel board patterns.

✄ Twenty-nine flannel board stories and patterns are found in *Storytelling with the Flannel Board* by Idalee Vonk (Minneapolis, MN: T.S. Denison & Company, Inc., 1983).

Frozen Fruit Pops

AGES: 3–6

GROUP SIZE:

3–6 children

DEVELOPMENTAL GOALS:

✄ To develop left-to-right progression

✄ To develop print awareness

LEARNING OBJECTIVE:

Following the recipe on a rebus chart, the children will make a healthy treat.

MATERIALS:

Frozen Fruit Pop rebus recipe (Appendix D3)
Copy paper
Laminator or clear contact paper
Unsweetened applesauce
Bowls
15 oz. can of fruit cocktail
Colander
5 oz. cups
Permanent marker
Two tablespoons
Tray
Spoons
Craft sticks
Aluminum foil

APPLE SAUCE

SKILL EXPLANATION:

Print awareness is developed as children understand that recipe directions are written. As children read the rebus chart, left-to-right progression is developed.

ADULT PREPARATION:

1. Make a copy of the Frozen Fruit Pop rebus recipe.
2. Laminate the recipe, or cover it with clear contact paper.
3. Wash hands.
4. Put unsweetened applesauce in a bowl.

continued

Frozen Fruit Pops continued

5. Open the can of fruit cocktail, drain and rinse in a colander, and then put the fruit in a bowl.
6. Write children's names on individual 5 oz. cups with a permanent marker.
7. Lay the recipe and tray on the table.
8. Place a tablespoon in each bowl.

ACTIVITY INTRODUCTION SUGGESTION:

"Frozen and fruit both start with |f|. Today we will read a recipe and make frozen fruit pops."

THEME INTRODUCTION SUGGESTION:

"Our unit is (summer fun) (healthy habits) (food). In the warm weather, we have fun eating cold treats. What is a cold healthy treat you like to eat in the summer? Today we will read a recipe and make frozen fruit pops. What is the first thing we do before cooking? Wash your hands with soap and water."

PROCEDURES:

The child will complete the following steps:
1. Wash hands.
2. Find the cup with his or her name.
3. Look at the rebus recipe chart.
4. Place 2 tablespoons of fruit in the cup.
5. Place 2 tablespoons of applesauce in the cup.
6. Stir the fruit and applesauce together.
7. Place a craft stick in the cup.
8. Place the cup on a tray.

The adult will complete the following steps:
1. Wash hands.
2. Cover each cup with aluminum foil.
3. Stick the craft stick through the center of the foil. This will ensure the stick stands up straight.

continued

Frozen Fruit Pops continued

4. Place the cups in the freezer overnight.
5. Serve to the children the next day for snack.

⚠ SAFETY PRECAUTION:

✄ Check for food allergies before beginning any food project.

✄ Supervise children closely when using small items such as the cut fruit in fruit cocktail to prevent a choking hazard.

BOOK SUGGESTION:

Blueberries for Sal by Robert McCloskey (New York: Viking Penguin, Inc., 1948). Sal gets separated from her mother as a baby cub is simultaneously separated from his as they all search for blueberries in this classic Caldecott Honor Book.

54

Great Gruff Goats' Position Words

SKILL EXPLANATION:

An appreciation of literacy and print awareness are developed as children listen to the adult read the book *The Three Billy Goats Gruff*. Vocabulary will be developed through the introduction and comprehension of spatial concepts (e.g., beside, under, on, between, or below).

ADULT PREPARATION:

1. Copy, color, and cut the patterns of the bridge, barn, river, Great Gruff Goats, and the troll.
2. Laminate the cutouts, or cover them with clear contact paper.
3. Cut sandpaper into strips.
4. Hot glue sandpaper to the back of the pieces.

ACTIVITY INTRODUCTION SUGGESTION:

"Today we are going to use some special flannel board pieces. We have a bridge, barn, river, goats, and a troll. I'm going to give you some special directions that I want you to follow."

THEME INTRODUCTION SUGGESTION:

"Our unit is *fairy tales*. Today our story is a fairy tale. Fairy tales are pretend stories where good always wins over things that are bad. After you listen to the story, tell me who is good and who needs to improve."

PROCEDURES:

The children will complete the following steps:

1. Listen to an adult read the story of the *Three Billy Goats Gruff*.
2. Place the troll, goats, and bridge on the flannel board.
3. Follow the adult's instructions to move the pieces:
   a. Put the goats **in** the barn.
   b. Put the river **beside** the barn.
   c. Put the bridge on **top** of the river.

continued

AGES: 3–6

GROUP SIZE:
2–4 children

DEVELOPMENTAL GOALS:
- ✂ To develop listening skills
- ✂ To develop spatial concepts

LEARNING OBJECTIVE:
Using flannel board pieces, the children will listen to a story and demonstrate the use of position words.

MATERIALS:
Bridge (Appendix A4)
Barn (Appendix A5)
River (Appendix A6)
Great Gruff Goats (Appendix A7)
Troll (Appendix A8)
Copy paper
Markers or colored pencils
Adult scissors
Lamination or clear contact paper
Hot glue gun
Hot glue gun sticks
Sandpaper
Book: *The Three Billy Goats Gruff*
Flannel board

G

55

Great Gruff Goats'
Position Words continued

d. Move the goats **outside** the barn.

e. The goats should be **beside** the bridge.

f. Put the smallest goat **in front of** the other two goats.

g. Put the middle-sized goat **between** the smallest and the largest goat.

h. Put the troll **under** the bridge but **above** the river.

i. Place the smallest goat **on** the bridge.

j. Move the middle-sized goat **behind** the smallest goat.

k. Move the middle-size goat and the smallest goat **beside** the bridge.

l. Move the biggest goat **below** the bridge.

m. Put the troll on the **bottom** of the river.

NOTE:

The directional words **right** and **left** may be used for older children. For example, in step 3b the direction "Put the river **right** of the barn" may be substituted. In step 3n, the direction "The goats should be to the **left** of the bridge" may be given.

EXPANSION:

Write the position words on index cards. When the direction involving the specific position word is given, show that word card.

BOOK SUGGESTION:

The Three Billy Goats Gruff by Paul Galdone (New York: Clarion Books, 1973) is the classic story of three goats searching for food and the troll who threatens the goats as they cross his bridge. The tale ends with the troll being tossed into the river.

Groovy Group Stories

G

SKILL EXPLANATION:

Print awareness is developed as children see the words they add to the story written by the adult. An essential component of group stories is the ability to listen and learn from classmates.

ADULT PREPARATION:

1. Write a story starter on a chart tablet or a large piece of paper such as *I am going to Grandma's house, and I'm going to take . . .*
2. Place a suitcase on the floor.

ACTIVITY INTRODUCTION SUGGESTION:

"Today we will work together to write a special story. Look at this chart. It says, 'I am going to Grandma's house, and I'm going to take . . .' Here is a suitcase on the floor. If you were going to Grandma's house, what is something you would like to take? Look around the room. Select what you'd like to take and bring it to the suitcase. We will add it to the story."

THEME INTRODUCTION SUGGESTION:

"Our unit is (family) (travel). Sometimes we have to travel to visit family. What would you pack to visit someone? Pretend we are going to take something from the class. We'll take turns putting things in the suitcase and we'll add it to the story."

PROCEDURES:

The children will complete the following steps:

1. Sit in a circle on the floor around the suitcase.
2. Listen to the adult read, *I am going to Grandma's house and I'm going to take. . . .*
3. Watch the adult open the suitcase and ask, "What would you take to Grandma's house? Look around the room, bring back something that you would pack to take with you."
4. Leave the circle and find something in the room that they would like to pack.
5. Sit in the circle holding the item.

continued

AGES: 3–6

GROUP SIZE:
6–16 children

DEVELOPMENTAL GOALS:
- ✂ To develop print awareness
- ✂ To enhance listening skills

LEARNING OBJECTIVE:
Using props, the children will create a group story.

MATERIALS:
Chart tablet or large piece of paper
Permanent marker
Suitcase

Groovy Group Stories continued

6. Take turns telling the others what their item is and why they would pack it.

7. Watch the adult write down what each child says.

8. Listen to the adult read the story (e.g., *I am going to Grandma's house and I'm going to take a puzzle so I have something to play with, a book to have something to read . . .*).

BOOK SUGGESTION:

The Relatives Came by Cynthia Rylant (New York: Bradbury Press, 1985). The relatives from Virginia come to visit. They eat, sleep, and enjoy each other's company.

Growing Up Picture Strip

AGES: 3–6

GROUP SIZE:
5 children

DEVELOPMENTAL GOALS:

✂ To develop print awareness

✂ To enhance vocabulary

LEARNING OBJECTIVE:

Using five pictures, glue, and strips of poster board, the child will dictate what is being shown in each picture.

MATERIALS:

Five pictures of a child at different ages
Copy paper
Adult scissors
Poster board
White school glue
Permanent fine-tipped marker

SKILL EXPLANATION:

Print awareness is developed as the child glues the pictures in a left-to-right progression. It is further enhanced when the child observes the adult writing down what is spoken.

ADULT PREPARATION:

1. Photocopy five pictures of a child at different ages. Make copies for each child.

2. Cut strips of poster board large enough to mount the pictures in a horizontal line.

ACTIVITY INTRODUCTION SUGGESTION:

"We have five pictures of a baby growing up. Which picture has the youngest baby? Put the pictures in order with the baby getting bigger and older in the next picture."

continued

Growing Up Picture Strip continued

THEME INTRODUCTION SUGGESTION:

"Our unit is (families) (babies) (all about me). What did you look like when you were a baby? Put the pictures in order and then tell me what the child is doing in each picture."

PROCEDURES:

The child will complete the following steps:

1. Place the pictures in sequential order from youngest to oldest.
2. Glue the pictures in order from left to right. Leave room to write under the pictures.
3. Dictate what the child is doing in each picture and watch the adult write the dictation under the appropriate picture.
4. Listen to the adult read what was written under each picture from left to right.

NOTE:

In place of using just one person's pictures, ask the children's families to send in five pictures of their child, showing that child at different ages. Photocopy the pictures and return the originals to the families.

EXPANSION:

Five- or six-year-olds may write their own descriptions under each picture.

BOOK SUGGESTION:

Big Sarah's Little Boots by Paulette Bourgeois (New York: Scholastic, Inc., 1987). Sarah outgrows the yellow boots she loves but tries to make them bigger through various antics. Finally, she gives them to her younger brother.

Hat Letter Toss

AGES: 3–6

GROUP SIZE:

2–4 children

DEVELOPMENTAL GOALS:

- ✄ To identify upper- and lowercase alphabet letters
- ✄ To coordinate muscles

LEARNING OBJECTIVE:

Using hats and bean bags, the child will identify alphabet letters.

MATERIALS:

4 baseball hats
Index cards
Permanent marker
Paper clips (large)
Bean bags
Basket

SKILL EXPLANATION:

Print awareness is developed as children identify the letters of the alphabet. This is strengthened through the use of large muscles, which enhances the retention of knowledge.

ADULT PREPARATION:

1. Select four alphabet letters for the children to identify. Write the letters on an index card with a permanent marker.

2. Use a large paper clip to attach the card to the inside of the cap's bill.

3. Lay the caps upside-down on the ground. The bills should face the child. Make sure the letters are right-side up as they face the child.

4. Place the bean bags in a basket.

ACTIVITY INTRODUCTION SUGGESTION:

"When do you wear a hat?" Show one of the hats. "What letter is on this hat? We are going to do a bean bag toss into the hats. Throw the bean bag into a hat and then tell me the name of the letter on the hat."

continued

Hat Letter Toss continued

THEME INTRODUCTION SUGGESTION:

"Our unit is (clothing) (winter) (sports) (wild west) (community helpers). Today we are going to talk about hats." Show one of the hats. "Who would wear this hat?" If the hats are different styles, show the children each hat and repeat the question. "Today we will toss a bean bag into the hats. When the bean bag lands in a hat, say the name of the letter on the hat."

PROCEDURES:

The child will complete the following steps:

1. Select a bean bag from the basket.
2. Toss the bean bag into a cap. Say the name of the letter attached to the cap, with adult assistance if needed. If the bean bag doesn't land in a cap, retrieve it and step closer to throw it again.
3. Alternate taking turns.

NOTE:

Set out a limited number of hats and alphabet letters. Too many letters will overwhelm the child. Use four letters when first introducing the activity. Add additional hats and letters as the skill level increases.

VARIATION:

Place alphabet letters on a bucket or plastic jar. Allow child to kneel on a chair and drop a clothespin into the bucket or jar. Identify the letter of the bucket or jar that the clothespin drops into.

BOOK SUGGESTION:

Caps for Sale by Esphyr Slobodkina. (New York: W. R. Scott, 1947). In this classic book a peddler who sells caps loses them all to monkeys, until he thinks of a plan to get them back.

Headband of Letters and Pictures

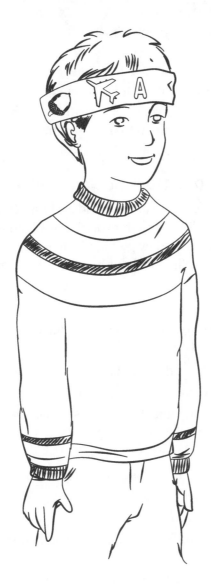

AGES: 3–5

GROUP SIZE:
2–4 children

DEVELOPMENTAL
GOALS:
✂ To identify alphabet
  letters
✂ To recognize
  beginning sounds

LEARNING
OBJECTIVE:
Using headbands, glue
and pictures, the
children will identify
letters and beginning
sounds.

MATERIALS:
Yellow construction
  paper
Adult scissors
Ruler
Broad tipped black
  marker
Magazines or clip art
Paper clip
Pencils
Stapler and staples
White school glue

SKILL EXPLANATION:

Phonics is presented in this activity as the child identifies the alphabet
letter and then sounds out a word, stressing the initial sound. The association between phonemes and graphemes is essential to help children
learn to decode words.

continued

Headband of Letters and Pictures continued

ADULT PREPARATION:

1. Cut 3"-wide strips of yellow construction paper to make a headband for each child.

2. Write an uppercase and matching lowercase letter on the middle of the headband. Use a different letter for each child.

3. Cut pictures from magazines or clip art for the beginning sound of each letter. Cut at least two to three pictures per letter.

4. Paper-clip pictures to each headband.

ACTIVITY INTRODUCTION SUGGESTION:

Show children the letter on a headband and ask, "What is this letter?" Repeat with all the different letters on the headbands. "Today we are going to make a headband by gluing pictures that start with that letter. After we are done, we'll model our headbands and guess our letters."

PROCEDURES:

The children will complete the following steps:

1. Select a headband.

2. Identify the letter on the headband.

3. Use a pencil to write name on the reverse side of the headband.

4. Remove the clip and glue the pictures to the headband, be careful not to glue over the letter.

5. Identify the pictures on the headband.

6. Identify the letter and the beginning sound in the pictures.

The adult will complete the following step:

1. Lay headbands flat to dry.

2. When the headband is dry, staple the headband to fit each child's head.

The children will complete the following steps:

1. Put the headband on with the letter showing in the front.

2. Sit in a circle.

3. Take turns standing; allow the others to say what pictures are on the headband.

continued

Headband of Letters
and Pictures continued

4. Identify beginning sound in the pictures.
5. Child will say the letter on his or her headband.
6. Repeat steps 3–5 until all children have had a turn.

⚠ SAFETY PRECAUTION:

Please supervise children closely when using small items such as paper clips to prevent choking hazards. In place of the paper clips, the strips and pictures may be placed in a bag for each child.

EXPANSION:

Children arrange themselves in alphabetical order, or stand together to spell words.

BOOK SUGGESTION:

Alphabet Under Construction by Denise Fleming (New York: Henry Holt & Co., 2002). Mouse builds the alphabet with different materials.

Hide and Seek High Frequency Words

AGES: 4–6

GROUP SIZE:

2–4 children

DEVELOPMENTAL GOALS:

✂ To identify words

✂ To develop visual discrimination

LEARNING OBJECTIVE:

Using rectangular word cards, poster board, and hook and loop tape, the children will identify and match words.

MATERIALS:

Poster board
Adult scissors
Permanent marker
Yardstick
Dolch words
   (Appendix B1)
Construction paper
Laminator or clear
   contact paper
Hook and loop tape
Masking tape

SKILL EXPLANATION:

Children will use their large muscles as they move around the room in search of words. Movement helps bring oxygen to the brain, which will aid in the retention of identifying and learning new words. Children use visual discrimination techniques as they match words on the poster board. Finding identical words helps the child develop fluency in reading.

ADULT PREPARATION:

1. Cut a poster board in half lengthwise. Save one half for future use.
2. Use a marker and a yardstick to draw a line down the middle of the half-sheet of poster board.
3. Divide the two columns into 3" rectangles.
4. Select high frequency words from the Dolch words (Appendix B1) to write in the left column. Write one word per rectangle.
5. Cut construction paper into the same-size rectangles that are on the poster board.
6. Write the same high frequency words on construction paper rectangles.
7. Laminate the rectangles, or cover them with clear contact paper.
8. Attach one side of hook and loop tape to the center back of the rectangles.
9. Attach the other side of the hook and loop tape to the center of the blank rectangles on the right side of the poster board.
10. Tape the poster board on the wall at the child's eye level.
11. Place the construction paper word cards around the room in sight and reach of the children.

ACTIVITY INTRODUCTION SUGGESTION:

"We are going to play hide-and-seek with words today. Look at the words on this chart. Now look around the room. These same words are hidden. Seek out one of these hidden words and bring it back to our chart."

continued

Hide and Seek High Frequency Words continued

THEME INTRODUCTION SUGGESTION:

"Our unit is *games.* How do you play hide and seek? Today the words are hiding. Look at the words on this chart. These are the words that are hidden. Look around the room, find a hidden word, and bring it back here."

PROCEDURES:

The children will complete the following steps:

1. Search and find a word card in the classroom.
2. Identify the word or the letters in the word, with adult assistance if needed.
3. Find the identical word on the poster board.
4. Attach the rectangle word to the poster board with the hook and loop tape.
5. Take turns repeating steps 1–4 matching all the words.

NOTE:

Pictures or photographs may be added to the word cards.

VARIATIONS:

✂ Make a miniature chart of high frequency words on copy paper. Copy a sheet for each child. As the child masters recognition of a word, allow him or her to place a sticker beside the word.

✂ Put hook and loop tape on both sides of the poster board. Create two sets of cards. Then the adult could change the words on the left to minimize the amount of poster board used.

BOOK SUGGESTIONS:

Little Quack's Hide and Seek by Lauren Thompson (New York: Simon & Schuster Books for Young Readers, 2004). Little Quack finds the best place to hide in the game he plays with his mama and siblings.

Ice Pop Writing

AGES: 3–6

GROUP SIZE:

3–6 children

DEVELOPMENTAL GOALS:

✂ To develop print awareness

✂ To enhance pre-writing skills

LEARNING OBJECTIVES:

Using frozen watercolor, the children will trace over their name

MATERIALS:

Ice cube tray
Liquid watercolor
Craft sticks
Construction paper
Pencil
Newspaper
Smocks

SKILL EXPLANATION:

Print awareness is developed as children see their names. Pre-writing skills are strengthened by tracing over each letter.

ADULT PREPARATION:

Day 1

1. Fill an ice cube tray with different colors of liquid watercolor.

2. Put a craft stick in each section.

3. Set the ice cube tray in the freezer overnight.

Day 2

1. Cover the table with newspaper.

2. Set paper with the penciled names on the table.

3. Loosen the cubes in the tray. Leave the cubes in the tray.

4. Set the tray with the colored cubes on the table.

ACTIVITY INTRODUCTION SUGGESTION:

What happens to ice when not in the freezer? As we write with these ice cubes, they will melt and leave a trail of color on the paper."

continued

Ice Pop Writing continued

THEME INTRODUCTION SUGGESTION:

"Our unit is *summer fun*. What do you do with ice pops? These ice pops are not the kind we eat. We write with these ice pops."

PROCEDURES:

The children will complete the following steps:

1. Put on smocks.

2. Select the paper with their name.

3. Hold a colored ice cube by the craft stick and trace over their name with the colored cube.

NOTE:

As the cube melts, it leaves a trail of color on the paper.

Ice Skating Words

AGES: 4–6

GROUP SIZE:

6 children

DEVELOPMENTAL GOALS:

✂ To identify rhyming words

✂ To develop large muscles

LEARNING OBJECTIVE:

Using paper plates, the children will find pictures that rhyme.

MATERIALS:

Copy Paper
Rhyming pictures (Appendices A9–A20)
  Ice (Appendix A9)
  Mice (Appendix A10)
  Mitten (Appendix A11)
  Kitten (Appendix A12)
  Hat (Appendix A13)
  Cat (Appendix A14)
  Coat (Appendix A15)
  Boat (Appendix A16)
  Pants (Appendix A17)
  Ants (Appendix A18)
  Fire (Appendix A19)
  Tire (Appendix A20)
Crayons, markers, or colored pencils
Scissors
Rubber cement
Paper plates
Bell

SKILL EXPLANATION:

Phonemic awareness is developed through the identification of the sounds in pictures that rhyme. Pairing this activity with the large muscle movement of pretending to skate will aid in the retention of the sounds of the words.

ADULT PREPARATION:

1. Copy the rhyming pictures in appendices A9–A20.

ACTIVITY INTRODUCTION SUGGESTION:

"We are going to pretend to skate. The paper plates will be our skates. When you skate you need a pair of skates. Find your pairs by finding the pictures that rhyme."

continued

70

Ice Skating Words continued

THEME INTRODUCTION SUGGESTION:

"Our unit is *winter*. What can you do outside when it is cold? We will pretend to ice skate on pictures that rhyme."

PROCEDURES:

The children will complete the following steps:

1. Identify the picture on each plate.
2. Put the plates together with the pictures that rhyme.
3. Give a pair of rhyming plates to each child.
4. Stand with one foot on each plate.
5. Pretend to skate on carpet with the rhyming plates.
6. Listen to the adult ring a bell and stop skating.
7. Mix the plates around.
8. Repeat steps 1–6.

NOTE:

The paper plates with pictures may be covered with clear contact paper to prevent shoes from scraping the picture off the plates.

Interview

GROUP SIZE:

4–6 children

DEVELOPMENTAL GOALS:

✃ To enhance listening skills

✃ To develop print awareness

LEARNING OBJECTIVE:

Using a microphone, the children will ask each other questions.

MATERIALS:

Construction paper
Markers
Masking tape
Small ball
Paper towel tube
Optional: Paint and brush, gems, sequins, rickrack, and glue

SKILL EXPLANATION:

An appreciation of literacy and print awareness are developed through listening to each other's questions and realizing the questions are written on the signs the adult is holding.

ADULT PREPARATION:

1. Using construction paper and markers, make individual signs with the following questions:

   a. What is your name?

   b. How old are you?

   c. What is your favorite food?

   d. Who do you live with?

   e. What is your favorite story?

2. Make a microphone by taping a small ball to the end of a paper towel tube.

3. Optional: Paint or decorate the microphone.

ACTIVITY INTRODUCTION SUGGESTION:

"Today we are going to take turns interviewing each other. What is an interview? It is when you ask a person questions to find out something you want to know."

THEME INTRODUCTION SUGGESTION:

"Our unit is (all about me) (community helpers). Sometimes you can interview someone about their job. People like fire fighters and police are called community helpers. Their jobs help a lot of people. What would be a question you would like to ask a policeman?"

PROCEDURES:

The children will complete the following steps:

1. Sit on the floor in a circle.

2. Look at the sign the adult is holding. Listen to the adult read the sign and then repeat what the adult said.

3. Listen to adult read the sign and ask the child sitting next to him or her, "What is your name?"

continued

Interview continued

4. The child answers and then takes the microphone and asks the child next to them, "What is your name?"

5. The microphone travels around the circle with each child taking a turn to ask and answer the question.

6. When the microphone returns to the adult, the adult may hold other signs and ask questions such as:

   a. How old are you?

   b. What is your favorite food?

   c. Who do you live with?

   d. What is your favorite story?

NOTE:

Use simple questions to introduce activity. As children become familiar with speaking in the group, use open-ended questions to encourage children to expand their answers, such as:

✄ How do you make your favorite food?

✄ What happens in your favorite story?

EXPANSIONS:

✄ Children may make their own microphones and interview each other.

✄ Microphones could be added to the dramatic play area and turn it into a stage or a newscaster's desk.

BOOK SUGGESTION:

Pig Pig Gets a Job by David McPhail (New York: Dutton Children's Books, 1990). Pig Pig thinks of all the different types of work he could do.

Jigsaw Puzzle

AGES: 3–5

GROUP SIZE:

2–4 children

DEVELOPMENTAL GOALS:

- ✄ To develop visual discrimination
- ✄ To associate the printed word with an object

LEARNING OBJECTIVE:

Using a puzzle guide and pieces, the child will put a puzzle together to create a picture and word.

MATERIALS:

Magazines
Adult scissors
Copy paper
Tag board
Rubber cement
Permanent marker

SKILL EXPLANATION:

As a child puts a puzzle together, he or she exhibits visual discrimination that expands into the ability to distinguish similar words. Once the puzzle is correctly put together, it will spell out a word for the child to identify promoting frequency.

ADULT PREPARATION:

1. Find a large picture in a magazine and cut it out.
2. Make a duplicate copy of the picture. This may be done in black and white. It will be used as a puzzle guide.

continued

Jigsaw Puzzle continued

3. Use rubber cement to glue the original picture on tag board.

4. Write the name of the object in the picture at the top of the construction paper.

5. When dry, cut the construction paper into puzzle pieces.

6. Glue the duplicate picture in the center of a piece of construction paper. Leave this puzzle guide whole.

ACTIVITY INTRODUCTION SUGGESTION:

"What is a jigsaw puzzle? It is one picture cut into smaller pieces that can be put back together. Today we are going to make a puzzle with a picture and a word. Once the puzzle is together, you'll be able to see the word."

THEME INTRODUCTION SUGGESTION:

"Our unit is [depends upon picture]. When you fit the pieces of the jigsaw back together, you'll see a picture of [name of picture]."

PROCEDURES:

The child will complete the following steps:

1. Identify the picture in the puzzle guide.

2. Place the puzzle pieces on the guide to re-create the picture.

3. Once the puzzle is complete, identify the word at the top of the puzzle.

NOTES:

✂ Clip art or coloring books may be used for pictures.

✂ Cut the number of puzzle pieces according to the child's ability. As the child becomes familiar with the puzzle, cut it into additional pieces to challenge him.

VARIATION:

Make a different puzzle for each child. Children may exchange puzzles and repeat the activity.

Job Dictation

AGES: 3–6

GROUP SIZE:

1–2 children

DEVELOPMENTAL GOALS:

✄ To promote print awareness

✄ To develop listening skills

LEARNING OBJECTIVE:

Using pictures of people doing their job, the child will dictate a story.

MATERIALS:

Newspapers or magazines
Adult scissors
Construction paper
Rubber cement
Pen or pencil
Paper

SKILL EXPLANATION:

A child will develop print awareness as he or she dictates and observes an adult write whatever he or she says. Literacy appreciation will further be developed as the child listens to the adult read what has been written.

ADULT PREPARATION:

1. Cut pictures of people doing various jobs out of newspapers or magazines. Use occupations children would be familiar with, such as a store clerk, mail carrier, trash collector, police officer, fire fighter, or doctor.

2. Glue the pictures on construction paper.

3. Write a story starter at the top of a sheet of paper for each child, *If I were a _____, I'd . . .*

ACTIVITY INTRODUCTION SUGGESTION:

"Today we will look at a picture of someone doing a certain job. You may tell me what you see happening in the picture and I will write it down. You'll be able to take this home and share it with your family."

THEME INTRODUCTION SUGGESTION:

"Our unit is *community helpers*. When someone does a job that helps people we call them community helpers. Doctors, grocers, mail carriers, and teachers are community helpers. Look at one of our pictures and tell me what the person is doing."

PROCEDURES:

The child will complete the following steps:

1. Select a picture of a person doing their job.

2. Dictate a story about that occupation by using the story starter *If I were a _____, I'd . . .*

3. Watch the adult write what is said and then listen as the adult reads it aloud.

continued

76

Job Dictation continued

NOTE:

Younger children may need more story prompts. They may also benefit from physical props to help them tell the story. Reading a story about a specific community helper may also provide assistance to create a story.

VARIATION:

Children may cut the pictures from magazines or bring cutout pictures from home.

BOOK SUGGESTION:

Career Day by Anne Rockwell (HarperCollins Publishers, 2000). It's career day at school, when the children bring special visitors to talk about their jobs.

Journals

AGES: 5–6

GROUP SIZE:

5–16 children

DEVELOPMENTAL GOALS:

✂ To practice writing

✂ To decode words

LEARNING OBJECTIVE:

Using a composition notebook, pencils, and colored pencils, the children will sound out words to write in a journal.

MATERIALS:

Composition notebook (Optional: several sheets of paper stapled together) Pencils and/or colored pencils

SKILL EXPLANATION:

The ability to write accompanies reading. As the children write, they will sound out needed words and practice matching letters with phonemes.

ADULT PREPARATION:

1. Make sure each child has a composition notebook, or staple several sheets of paper together.

2. Designate a time each day for journal writing.

ACTIVITY INTRODUCTION SUGGESTION:

"Today we are going to start writing in our journals. A journal is a book put together with blank or lined paper. We will write in our journals everyday. Sometimes I will tell you what to write about. Other times you will be able to write about anything you'd like."

THEME INTRODUCTION SUGGESTION:

"Our unit is *all about me*. Today we will write in our journals all about ourselves."

PROCEDURES:

The children will complete the following steps:

1. Attempt to sound out words when writing in journal.

2. Draw picture to go along with words.

NOTE:

To begin journal writing, the adult may need to give suggestions or story starters. As children become more familiar with the task, they may choose their own topics.

BOOK SUGGESTION:

Arthur Writes a Story by Marc Brown (New York: Little, Brown & Co., 1996). Arthur's imagination goes wild as he writes a story for school.

78

Jump Words

AGES: 4–6

GROUP SIZE:
2–4 children

DEVELOPMENTAL GOALS:
✁ To identify words
✁ To develop gross motor muscles

LEARNING OBJECTIVE:
Using construction paper words and a tablecloth, the child will identify and jump to specific words.

MATERIALS:
54" square vinyl tablecloth with flannel backing
Ruler
Permanent marker
Index cards
Basket
Masking tape

SKILL EXPLANATION:

Fluency will be developed as children identify words. These words will have a greater likelihood of being retained when accompanied by the use of large muscles when jumping.

ADULT PREPARATION:

1. Draw 12" × 12" squares on the tablecloth with a permanent marker.
2. Write one word or one alphabet letter in each square.
3. Make duplicate copies of words or alphabet letters on index cards.
4. Place the words in a basket.
5. Place the tablecloth on the floor. Secure with masking tape.

continued

Jump Words continued

ACTIVITY INTRODUCTION SUGGESTION:

"Today we are going to play a jumping game. Look at the cloth. What is written on it? In the basket are letters. We will take turns pulling a letter from the basket. Look at the letter. Find the same letter on the cloth and then jump to that letter." The adult may demonstrate.

THEME INTRODUCTION SUGGESTION:

"Our unit is *Olympics*. The Olympics are special games that people from all over the world are able to participate. One of the events in the Olympics is the long-jump. Today we are going to pretend we are doing the long jump to an alphabet letter."

PROCEDURES:

The child will complete the following steps:

1. Select and identify a word from the basket.
2. Locate the word on the tablecloth.
3. Jump from the edge of the tablecloth to that word.
4. Place the word card back in the basket and sit down.
5. Take turns repeating steps 1–4.

NOTE:

Use alphabet letters in place of words for younger children.

SAFETY PRECAUTION:

Use the masking tape to secure the tablecloth to the ground to prevent it from slipping when the children jump.

BOOK SUGGESTION:

Jump, Frog, Jump! by Robert Kalan (New York: Greenwillow, 1995). Frog continually hops out of danger as children enjoy repeating the phrase, "Jump, frog, jump!"

Key Words

AGES: 4–6

SKILL EXPLANATION:

Fluency will be enhanced as children identify common words. Visual discrimination will allow the children to look at all the letters in the word to find its match. Seeing and reading the word twice will further influence frequency.

ADULT PREPARATION:

1. Trace multiple key and car patterns onto construction paper, and then cut them out.
2. Select words from the high frequency word list (Appendix B1).
3. Write each word on one car and one key.
4. Laminate the key and car patterns, or cover them with clear contact paper.
5. Place cars in a horizontal line on the table.
6. Put keys in a small basket.

ACTIVITY INTRODUCTION SUGGESTION:

Hold up the key pattern and ask, "What is this?" Then hold up the car pattern and ask, "How do these two things go together? You need a key to start most cars. On each car and key that goes together we have written the same word. You will need to find the keys and cars that match."

THEME INTRODUCTION SUGGESTION:

"Our unit is *transportation*. A car is transportation. It helps us get from one place to another. What is another means of transportation that enables us to get from place to place?"

PROCEDURES:

The children will take turns to complete the following steps:

1. Select a key out of the basket.
2. Identify the word on the key, with adult assistance if necessary.
3. Find the identical word on the car.
4. Lay the key on the matching car.
5. Repeat steps 1–4 until all keys and cars have been matched.

GROUP SIZE:
2–4 children

DEVELOPMENTAL GOALS:
✄ To identify high frequency words
✄ To develop visual discrimination

LEARNING OBJECTIVE:
Using car and key cutouts, the children will match words.

MATERIALS:
Pencil or pen
Car pattern (Appendix A21)
Key pattern (Appendix A22)
Construction paper
Adult scissors
Dolch words (Appendix B1)
Permanent marker
Laminator or clear contact paper
Basket

continued

NOTES:

✂ Some children will simply look for the matching beginning letter.

✂ For younger children, color code the cars and keys using the alphabet. (e.g., uppercase *A* on a red car, and lowercase *a* on a red key).

Keyboard Match

K

AGES: 3–6

GROUP SIZE:
1–2 children

DEVELOPMENTAL GOALS:
- ✄ To identify alphabet letters
- ✄ To develop eye-hand coordination

LEARNING OBJECTIVE:
Using a computer keyboard and stickers, the child will match alphabet letters.

MATERIALS:
Computer keyboard
Permanent marker
Removable stickers

SKILL EXPLANATION:

Through the identification and matching of alphabet letters, the child will develop an appreciation of print.

ADULT PREPARATION:

1. Using a permanent marker, write uppercase letters on the removable stickers.
2. Set the keyboard on the table.

ACTIVITY INTRODUCTION SUGGESTION:

"Today we are going to use our computer keyboard and stickers to play a letter-matching game. First pick a sticker. What letter is on that sticker? Find the same letter on the keyboard. Place the sticker on the same letter."

THEME INTRODUCTION SUGGESTION:

"Our unit is *community helpers*. Many people in our community work at jobs that require a computer. These people have to type things so they have to know all their letters and where they are found on the keyboard."

continued

Keyboard Match continued

PROCEDURES:

The child will complete the following steps:

1. Select and identify the letter on one sticker.

2. Find the identical letter on the keyboard.

3. Place the letter on the matching key.

4. Repeat steps 1–3 until all keyboard letters have been covered with the matching sticker.

EXPANSION:

Write a different word in each row of stickers. Write one letter on each sticker to spell out the word (e.g., in one row write *c-a-t*).

Kite Visual Discrimination

SKILL EXPLANATION:

The ability to visually discriminate between objects transfers to the ability to recognize the different letters and the order of these letters in words.

ADULT PREPARATION:

1. Copy and cut multiple copies of the kite pattern onto construction paper.
2. Color pairs of the kites with identical colors or designs.
3. Cut a 5" length of string for each kite.
4. Staple the string to the bottom of the kites.
5. Tape one set of kites to the wall or windows.
6. Place the second set of kites in a basket.

ACTIVITY INTRODUCTION SUGGESTION:

Hold up a kite. "What is this? When the weather is windy, people will have a string attached to their kite, and they will go outside in an open place and let their kite fly in the wind. Each person will pick a kite from the basket, and then they will look carefully at the kites on the wall. Find the kite that is the same."

THEME INTRODUCTION SUGGESTION:

"Our unit is (weather) (March). People often fly kites during the windy month of March. We have kites on the wall. Each kite has a match. Look at the kites in the basket. Match up the kites from the basket with the kites on the wall."

PROCEDURES:

The children will complete the following steps:

1. Sit in a circle or semicircle.
2. Select a kite from the basket.
3. "Fly" around the room to find the matching kite.
4. Take the matching kite from the wall or window.
5. Return to the circle or semicircle with the matching kites.

continued

K

AGES: 3–6

GROUP SIZE:
2–6 children

DEVELOPMENTAL GOALS:

- ✂ To practice visual discrimination
- ✂ To classify objects through matching

LEARNING OBJECTIVE:

Using kite cutouts, the children will match identical objects.

MATERIALS:

Kite pattern (Appendix A23)
Construction paper
Adult scissors
Crayons, markers, or colored pencils
String
Ruler
Stapler and staples
Masking tape
Basket

85

Kite Visual Discrimination continued

VARIATION:

As an outside activity, clip one set of kites to a fence using clothespins.

BOOK SUGGESTION:

Curious George Flies a Kite by Margret Rey, illustrated by H. A. Rey. (Boston: Houghton Mifflin Company, 1958). George gets into trouble as usual. This book is 80 pages. The episode with the kite starts on page 50. For younger children and children with shorter attention spans, the book may be read in segments.

Label Match

AGES: 3–6

GROUP SIZE:

2–4 children

DEVELOPMENTAL GOALS:

✄ To develop print awareness

✄ To identify familiar symbols

LEARNING OBJECTIVE:

Using labels of familiar objects, the child will find matching pairs.

MATERIALS:

Labels of familiar objects from cans, boxes, or bags
Construction paper
Adult scissors
Rubber cement

SKILL EXPLANATION:

When identifying familiar labels, the child is demonstrating print awareness and reading readiness. The ability to recognize a well-known product will transfer to the recognition of words.

ADULT PREPARATION:

1. Collect matching labels from cans, boxes, or bags of items that are familiar to children.

2. Cut construction paper into pieces and glue the labels on the paper, creating cards.

3. Arrange the cards on the table face down.

ACTIVITY INTRODUCTION SUGGESTION:

Hold up several different labels one at a time. After showing each label, ask, "What is this? Today we are going to play a matching game. We will lay the labels on the table so we cannot see the label. Please turn over two labels. If they are the same, take both labels out. If they are not the same, turn them back over. We will take turns trying to find matches."

continued

Label Match continued

THEME INTRODUCTION SUGGESTION:

"Our unit is (health) (nutrition) (food). We need to eat healthy food in order to grow. Today we are going to match our food labels."

PROCEDURES:

The child will complete the following steps:

1. Turn two cards face up.
2. Identify the label on the cards.
3. If the cards are identical, leave in position.
4. If the cards are different, turn them face down again.
5. Repeat steps 1–4 until all cards have been matched and are face up.

VARIATION:

Matching coupons may be used in place of labels.

BOOK SUGGESTION:

Gregory, the Terrible Eater by Mitchell Sharmat (New York, Scholastic, Inc., 1980). Gregory, the goat, doesn't want the food his parents offer. He craves human food until his parents learn to introduce "goat" food slowly into his diet.

88

Lemon Juice Writing

SKILL EXPLANATION:

Fluency is enhanced as children recognize words. Print awareness is developed as children recognize alphabet letters. Reading and writing are mutually beneficial activities.

ADULT PREPARATION:

1. Copy the family letter (Appendix B4).
2. Write *I love you* on a strip of paper.
3. Put lemon juice in small plastic cups.

ACTIVITY INTRODUCTION SUGGESTION:

"What do you use when you write? Today we are going to write a secret message with lemon juice."

THEME INTRODUCTION SUGGESTION:

This week's unit is *the five senses.* Today we will write a message that we won't be able to see until it dries."

PROCEDURES:

The children will complete the following steps:

1. Write their names on individual sheets of white construction paper with a pencil.
2. Dip a cotton swab into the lemon juice.
3. Look at the words on the strip of paper.
4. Identify the letters and the words.
5. Write *I love you* with the lemon juice and cotton swab.
6. Set the paper to the side to dry.
7. Once the paper is dry, take it home with the family note instructing the family to iron the paper.

NOTE:

The lemon juice will dry and become invisible. Heat from a low iron will turn the writing a light brown. The family will be able to then read the message.

AGES: 4–6

GROUP SIZE:

4–6 children

DEVELOPMENTAL GOALS:

✄ To develop print awareness

✄ To enhance fine motor control

LEARNING OBJECTIVES:

Using lemon juice and cotton swabs, the children will recognize words and write a message.

MATERIALS:

Copy paper
Family Letter 2 (Appendix B4)
Marker
Strip of paper
Lemon juice
Small plastic cups
Smocks
White construction paper
Pencil
Cotton swabs

Letter Bag

AGES: 3–6

GROUP SIZE:

1–20 children

DEVELOPMENTAL
GOALS:

✕ To recognize
   alphabet letters

✕ To associate the
   printed word with
   objects

LEARNING
OBJECTIVE:

Using a paper bag and
objects from home, the
child will find objects
that begin with a
specific alphabet letter.

MATERIALS:

Family Letter 3
   (Appendix B5)
Paper grocery bag
Marker
Objects from home
Dry erase board or
   large sheet of paper
Dry erase marker

SKILL EXPLANATION:

Phonics are demonstrated through the association of a letter and an
object's initial sound. Print awareness is enhanced as the child identifies
the alphabet letter and word the adult writes.

ADULT PREPARATION:

1. Explain the letter bag during parent orientation. Write an alphabet
   letter on the paper grocery bag.

2. Select a child to send the letter bag home with. Write the child's
   name on the bag. Duplicate and send a letter home to the child's
   family reminding them of the letter bag concept (Appendix B5).

ACTIVITY INTRODUCTION SUGGESTION (DAY 1):

"Today _____ will take the letter bag home. What is the letter
written on the bag? _____ will find things at home that start
with this letter and bring them to school tomorrow."

PROCEDURES:

At home, the child will complete the following steps:

1. Select items that begin with the letter written on the bag, with family
   help if necessary.

2. Put the items in the bag and return to school.

ACTIVITY INTRODUCTION SUGGESTION (DAY 2):

"Today we are going to look inside the letter bag that _____
brought. What is the letter written on the bag?" The children will
complete the following steps:

1. Sit in a circle or semicircle.

2. Watch the child who brought the letter bag pull items out of the
   letter bag one at a time and identify each item.

3. Observe the adult write down the words of the items on a dry erase
   board or a large piece of paper as the items are pulled out of the bag.

4. Once all the items have been shown, repeat the words after the
   adult.

continued

Letter Bag continued

NOTES:

- ✄ A smaller bag may be used to limit the size and number of items put in the bag.

- ✄ It's best to use paper bags or containers that are replaceable in case a child is absent. Then the letter bag may still go home with the next person.

- ✄ The letter bag may be sent home daily or weekly.

Letter Walk

AGES: 4–6

GROUP SIZE:

6–20 children

DEVELOPMENTAL GOALS:

✄ To identify an alphabet letter

✄ To identify objects that begin with a specific letter sound

LEARNING OBJECTIVE:

Using a letter written on construction paper, the children will find objects in their environment that start with that letter.

MATERIALS:

Marker
Small sheet of construction paper or index card

SKILL EXPLANATION:

Children will practice phonemic awareness as they sound out the words of objects they see on their walk. Phonics is incorporated by the association of matching the initial sound of a word to a specific written letter.

ADULT PREPARATION:

1. Select a letter to search for on the letter walk.
2. Write the uppercase and lowercase letter on a small sheet of construction paper or index card, one for each child to hold as a reference.

ACTIVITY INTRODUCTION SUGGESTION:

"Today we are going on a letter walk." Hold up the letter and ask, "What is this letter?" Say the letter with the children then ask, "What sound does this letter make?" Make the sound with the children then say, "As we walk let's look around and name the things that start with that sound and letter."

THEME INTRODUCTION SUGGESTION:

"Our unit is *transportation*. Walking is a means of transportation. It is one way to go from one place to another. Today we are going on a letter walk to find things that start with this letter." Hold up letter.

continued

Letter Walk continued

PROCEDURES:

The children will complete the following steps:

1. Identify the letter on the small sheet of construction paper or index card.

2. Make the sound or sounds associated with that letter.

3. Walk with the adult either around the building or outside.

4. Search and identify items that begin with the specified letter sound.

BOOK SUGGESTION:

I Went Walking by Sue Williams, illustrated by Julie Vivas. (New York: Trumpet Club, 1989). A child goes for a walk and hears, "What did you see?" Children will enjoy repeating this repetitive phrase.

Magic Names

AGES: 3–6

GROUP SIZE:

2 children

DEVELOPMENTAL GOALS:

✂ To identify classmates' names

✂ To develop writing skills

LEARNING OBJECTIVE:

Using carbon paper, copy paper, paper clips, and pencils, the child will write on two sheets of paper.

MATERIALS:

Copy paper
Permanent marker
Carbon paper
Paper clips
Pencils

SKILL EXPLANATION:

Fluency is developed through the identification of familiar names. Reading accompanied by writing aids retention of the names.

ADULT PREPARATION:

1. Print a list of the names of the children in the class.
2. Put a sheet of carbon paper in between two sheets of copy paper; attach the papers together with paper clips. Make two sets of these.
3. Set carbon sets on the table with the carbon side facing down.
4. Place the class list between the carbon sets.

ACTIVITY INTRODUCTION SUGGESTION:

"Today we are going to write names on magic paper. When we write or draw on one piece of paper, the magic of this paper will cause it to write the same thing on another piece of paper at the same time!"

THEME INTRODUCTION SUGGESTION:

"Our unit is *circus*. Sometimes we see magicians in the circus. A magician performs tricks and people do not know how he does his tricks. Just like today. You will write on one piece of paper and have it show up on two pieces of paper like magic!"

continued

94

Magic Names continued

PROCEDURES:

The child will complete the following steps:

1. Find his or her name on the class list, with adult assistance if necessary.

2. Write his or her name at the top of the carbon set with a pencil.

3. Identify other classmates' names, with adult assistance if necessary.

4. Write other classmates' names on the carbon set with a pencil.

5. When finished, remove the paper clips; look at both sheets of paper to see that they now have two sheets written, the original and the carbon.

The adult will complete the following step:

1. Explain to the child that before there were copy machines or computers and printers, people used to make copies of their writing using carbon paper.

NOTE:

Carbon paper may be found at office supply stores.

BOOK SUGGESTION:

Milo's Hat Trick by Jon Agee (New York: Hyperion Books for Children, 2001) Milo is a magician who finds a bear to pull out of his hat.

Magnetic Word Match

AGES: 4–6

GROUP SIZE:

2–4 children

DEVELOPMENTAL GOALS:

✂ To identify words

✂ To practice visual discrimination

LEARNING OBJECTIVE:

Using magnetic words and a metal baking sheet, the child will identify and match words.

MATERIALS:

Dolch words (Appendix B1)
3½" × 5" plain index cards
Adult scissors
Permanent marker
Magnetic tape
Metal baking sheet
Small container

SKILL EXPLANATION:

Fluency is enhanced through the identification of words. Visual discrimination aids the child in finding the identical word.

ADULT PREPARATION:

1. Select words from Appendix B1.
2. Cut index cards in half.
3. Write duplicate words on individual index card pieces.
4. Cut index card pieces into circles ("cookies").
5. Place a strip of magnetic tape on the back of each word.
6. Place one set of magnetic words on the metal baking sheet in a vertical column on the left side of the baking sheet.
7. Put the other set in a small container.

ACTIVITY INTRODUCTION SUGGESTION:

"What do you put on a baking sheet? Today we will match words on this baking sheet. We need two of each word."

THEME INTRODUCTION SUGGESTION:

"Our unit is *baking*. The word cards are shaped like cookies, which are cooked on a baking sheet."

continued

Magnetic Word Match continued

Note: This activity would work with other units, depending upon the shape of the word card (e.g., a leaf shape during the Fall unit, a turkey for Thanksgiving, etc.).

PROCEDURES:

The child will complete the following steps:

1. Identify the words on the baking sheet, with adult assistance if needed.
2. Select another magnetic word card out of the small container.
3. Identify the word and match it with the same word on the baking sheet.
4. Place the second magnetic word to the right of the first word.
5. Repeat steps 2–4 until all words have been matched creating a second column identical to the first.

NOTE:

Magnetic tape may be bought in which one side may be peeled and stuck to the card.

VARIATION:

Spelling may be practiced by placing word cards in one column and then using plastic magnetic letters to spell out the words on the card.

BOOK SUGGESTION:

Pizza Party! by Grace Maccarone (New York: Scholastic, Inc., 1994). Children make a pizza from scratch in this beginning reader.

Mirror Writing

AGES: 3–6

GROUP SIZE:

Individual

DEVELOPMENTAL GOALS:

- ✂ To develop writing skills
- ✂ To identify alphabet letters

LEARNING OBJECTIVE:

Using window markers, a mirror, and an alphabet strip, the child will write alphabet letters.

MATERIALS:

Permanent marker
Strip of paper
Masking tape
Full-length mirror
Smock
Window markers

SKILL EXPLANATION:

Holding the marker up to write on the mirror will encourage large muscle development. Pairing alphabet recognition with a large motor activity will aid in the retention of letter identification.

ADULT PREPARATION:

1. Write selected lowercase letters on a strip of paper with the permanent marker.
2. Tape the paper to a full-length mirror.

ACTIVITY INTRODUCTION SUGGESTION:

"Today instead of writing our letters on paper, we are going to use special markers and practice writing on a mirror."

continued

98

Mirror Writing continued

THEME INTRODUCTION SUGGESTION:

"Our unit is *all about me*. What do you see when you look in a mirror? You may look at yourself while you practice writing."

PROCEDURES:

The child will complete the following steps:

1. Put on a smock.
2. Look at the alphabet letters on the mirror.
3. Using window markers, duplicate the selected lowercase letters on the mirror.
4. Identify the letters as they are written.

NOTES:

✂ Window markers may be purchased from a school supply or toy store.

✂ The mirror may be cleaned with a glass cleaner.

VARIATIONS:

✂ Older children may trace the outline of their face and then write their name on the mirror.

✂ Children may write on windows.

N

GROUP SIZE:

2–4 children

DEVELOPMENTAL GOALS:

✄ To recognize an alphabet letter

✄ To promote fine motor control

LEARNING OBJECTIVE:

Using construction paper, newspaper, pen or pencil, child-size safety scissors, and glue, the child will recognize a specific alphabet letter.

MATERIALS:

Permanent marker
Construction paper
Newspaper
Adult scissors
Pen or pencil
Child-size safety
    scissors
White school glue

Newspaper Letter Hunt

SKILL EXPLANATION:

An appreciation of literacy and print awareness are developed through the use of reading material, such as a newspaper. Pairing the child's motor activities with the recognition of a specific alphabet letter will assist the child in learning the letter.

ADULT PREPARATION:

1. Select one alphabet letter and write the lower- and uppercase letter at the top of the construction paper for each child.

2. Cut the newspaper into ¼ sheets that will be easier for the children to handle.

ACTIVITY INTRODUCTION SUGGESTION:

Hold up the newspaper and ask, "What is this? There are some people whose job is to write things in the newspaper so we can read about things that are happening everyday. Today I have cut the newspaper into smaller pieces." Show the letter written on construction paper and ask, "What is this letter? We are going to use a pencil to circle the letter ____, then we will cut the letter out and glue it on the construction paper."

continued

Newspaper Letter Hunt continued

THEME INTRODUCTION SUGGESTION:

"Our unit is (communications) (community helpers). Some people have jobs where they write for the newspaper as a way to communicate. The newspaper tells us what is happening in our community and in the world. The newspaper is made up of real stories, which are made up from words, which are made from letters. Today we are looking for the letter _____. We are going to circle the letter, and then cut it out and glue it on the construction paper."

PROCEDURES:

The child will complete the following steps:

1. Identify the letter on the construction paper.
2. Circle the same letter in the newspaper.
3. Cut out the words containing the circled letter.
4. Glue the words on the sheet of construction paper with the written letter.
5. Wash hands.

NOTES:

✄ The adult may cut out headlines for the child to look through to find the selected alphabet letter.

✄ If ¼ page of the newspaper seems overwhelming for the children, cut out a smaller section. Give the children a specific number of letters to circle.

BOOK SUGGESTION:

The Furry News: How to Make a Newspaper by Loreen Leedy (New York: Holiday House, 1990). The animals work together to create a newspaper in this *Reading Rainbow Book*. It includes suggestions for making a family, neighborhood, or school newspaper.

Number Word Recognition

SKILL EXPLANATION:

Fluency is used in the recognition of the number word. The child demonstrates comprehension when they are able to pair the word with the matching numeral.

ADULT PREPARATION:

1. Cut tag board into 8" × 3" strips.
2. Write one number word (one to ten) on the left side of the strip.
3. On the right side of the strip, write the corresponding numeral.
4. Cut the strips into two pieces using zigzag or puzzle intersecting cuts, which will separate the number word and numeral.
5. Scatter the number word sets one to five on the table.
6. Place the number word sets six to ten to the side.

ACTIVITY INTRODUCTION SUGGESTION:

"Today we are going to match numbers to their words." Hold up a matching number and word. "We have the number on one card and its word on the other card. If they match, the two pieces will fit together like a puzzle."

PROCEDURES:

The child will complete the following steps:

1. Select the number words and set them in a vertical row.
2. Identify the number words, with adult help if necessary.
3. Find the numeral 1.
4. Match it to the word *one*. If correct, the pieces will fit together.
5. Continue steps 3–4 with the number words and numerals two to five.
6. If successful, set the number word sets one to five to the side.
7. Repeat steps 1–5 with the number word sets six to ten.

AGES: 4–6

GROUP SIZE:
2–4 children

DEVELOPMENTAL GOALS:
✂ To identify number words
✂ To identify numerals

LEARNING OBJECTIVE:
Using number words and numerals, the child will identify and match the word to the numeral.

MATERIALS:
Tag board
Ruler
Pencil
Adult scissors
Permanent marker

continued

Number Word Recognition continued

NOTE:

When number words are first introduced, place stickers equal to the number under the word (e.g., two stickers under the word *two*).

BOOK SUGGESTION:

Boom Chicka Rock by John Archambault (New York: Scholastic, Inc., 2004). Mice named after the hours of a clock search for birthday cake in this rhyming text.

Nursery Rhymes

AGES: 4–6

GROUP SIZE:

2–16 children

DEVELOPMENTAL GOALS:

- ✂ To develop listening skills
- ✂ To identify rhyming words

LEARNING OBJECTIVE:

Using nursery rhyme tag boards, a candlestick, a large plastic tub, a small pail, and individual kazoos, the children will act out and listen to nursery rhymes as they identify rhyming words.

MATERIALS:

Mother Goose Nursery Rhyme book
Tag board sheets
Permanent marker
Pattern of Jack Be Nimble (Appendix A24)
Pattern of Rub-a Dub-Dub, Three Men in a Tub (Appendix A25)
Pattern of Jack and Jill (Appendix A26)

SKILL EXPLANATION:

An appreciation of literacy is developed through listening to Mother Goose. Phonemic awareness is demonstrated through sounding out rhyming words.

ADULT PREPARATION:

1. Use a Mother Goose Nursery Rhyme book; copy the words to the following on individual sheets of tag board. Leave room to glue the pattern on the board.
   a. Jack Be Nimble
   b. Rub-a Dub-Dub, Three Men in a Tub
   c. Jack and Jill
   d. Little Boy Blue Come Blow Your Horn
2. Copy, cut, and color the patterns of Jack Be Nimble, Rub-a Dub-Dub, Three Men in a Tub, Jack and Jill, and Little Boy Blue Come Blow Your Horn.
3. Use rubber cement to glue the cutouts on the appropriate nursery rhyme tag board.

continued

Nursery Rhymes continued

4. Set up different stations in the room with the following items:

   a. A candlestick and the Jack Be Nimble tag board

   b. A large plastic tub and the Rub-a Dub-Dub tag board

   c. A small pail and the Jack and Jill tag board

   d. Individual kazoos and the Little Boy Blue Come Blow Your Horn tag board

MATERIALS:

Pattern of Little Boy
   Blue Come Blow
   Your Horn
   (Appendix A27)
Copy paper
Markers, colored
   pencils, or crayons
Adult scissors
Rubber cement
Candlestick
Large plastic tub
Small pail
Kazoos

ACTIVITY INTRODUCTION SUGGESTION:

"We are going to listen to and act out nursery rhymes. In a nursery rhyme, the words rhyme at the end of the line." Hold up poster of Jack be Nimble. "Let's say this together. Jack be nimble. Jack be quick. Jack jump over the candle _____." Leave off the last word to see if children are able to rhyme. If not, supply the word—*stick*—for them.

THEME INTRODUCTION SUGGESTION:

"Our unit is *nursery rhymes*. In a nursery rhyme, words rhyme at the end of the line. We are going to listen to and act out some nursery rhymes from Mother Goose."

PROCEDURES:

The children will complete the following steps:

1. Visit the different areas of the room and listen to the following nursery rhymes as they are read from the tag board sheets:

   ✂ Jack Be Nimble

   ✂ Rub a Dub-Dub, Three Men in a Tub

   ✂ Jack and Jill

   ✂ Little Boy Blue Come Blow Your Horn

2. Identify the rhyming words after each nursery rhyme is heard.

3. Take turns to:

   ✂ Jump over Jack's candlestick.

   ✂ Sit together in a large round tub as the three men in a tub.

   ✂ Pretend to gather water and "fall down the hill" like Jack and Jill.

   ✂ Blow an individual kazoo like Little Boy Blue.

continued

Nursery Rhymes continued

NOTE:

Each nursery rhyme activity may be done on separate days rather than rotating through all of them on a given day.

BOOK SUGGESTIONS:

- ✂ *Sylvia Long's Mother Goose* by Sylvia Long (San Francisco: Chronicle Books, 1999). An assortment of familiar Mother Goose rhymes.
- ✂ *Tomie de Paola's Mother Goose* by Tomie de Paola (New York: G.P. Putnam's Sons, 1985). A collection of 204 Mother Goose nursery rhymes.
- ✂ *The Real Mother Goose* by G. W. Wright (Chicago: Rand McNally & Company, 1916). This classic book contains over 300 nursery rhymes.
- ✂ *Mary Had a Little Jam and Other Silly Rhymes* by Bruce Lansky (New York: Meadowbrook Press, 2004). This book was formerly called *The New Adventures of Mother Goose,* as it takes the original characters and rewrites their poems.

Obstacle Letter Search

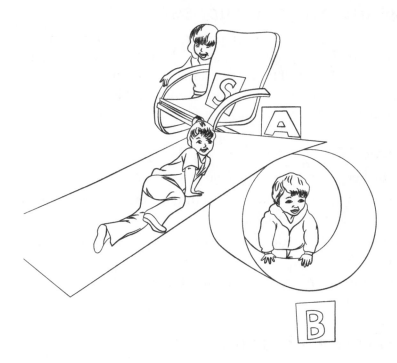

AGES: 3–6

GROUP SIZE:
2–4 children

DEVELOPMENTAL GOALS:
- ✂ To identify alphabet letters
- ✂ To stimulate cognitive abilities through gross motor involvement

LEARNING OBJECTIVE:
Using alphabet letters and an obstacle course, the children will crawl or climb as they identify letters or words.

MATERIALS:
Chairs
Tables
Index cards
Permanent marker
Laminator or clear contact paper
Masking tape

SKILL EXPLANATION:

Print awareness is expanded through the identification of alphabet letters. The cross lateral movement associated with crawling will aid in the retention of learning alphabet letters.

ADULT PREPARATION:

1. Set up an obstacle course that will encourage children to crawl or climb (e.g., over chairs, under tables).
2. Select the alphabet letters the children will identify.
3. Write the letters on index cards with a permanent marker.
4. Laminate the letter cards, or cover them with clear contact paper.
5. Use masking tape to fix the letter cards throughout the obstacle course.

ACTIVITY INTRODUCTION SUGGESTION:

"We are going to go through an obstacle course. As we go through the different areas, we are searching for letters. When you find a letter, call out its name."

continued

Obstacle Letter Search continued

THEME INTRODUCTION SUGGESTION:

"Our unit is *Olympics*. The Olympics are games that people from all over the world come and participate in. We are going to have our own Olympic game. We will have an obstacle course. You will have to crawl and climb through each area to find the alphabet letters. When you find one, call out its name."

PROCEDURES:

The children will complete the following steps:

1. Take turns climbing and crawling through the obstacle course, with adult assistance if needed.
2. Identify the letter, with adult assistance if needed, as they climb or crawl over it.
3. Once through the course, wait their turn to go through the obstacle course again.

SAFETY PRECAUTION:

Use heavy wooden chairs for children to climb over.

VARIATION:

Use high frequency words in place of letters.

BOOK SUGGESTION:

Olympics! by Barbara G. Hennessy (New York: Penguin Group, 1996). This book presents a brief synopsis of the Olympics from the preparation to the events.

Outdoor Writing

AGES: 3–6

GROUP SIZE:
2–16 children

DEVELOPMENTAL GOALS:

✄ To develop writing skills

✄ To hold a writing instrument correctly

LEARNING OBJECTIVE:
Using a plastic cup with water and a small paintbrush, the children will write outdoors.

MATERIALS:
Plastic cups
Water
Small paintbrushes
Tray
Pitcher

SKILL EXPLANATION:

Print awareness is increased as children realize their movements create marks that expand into the development of words.

ADULT PREPARATION:

1. Fill a plastic cup ⅔ full of water for each child.
2. Set a small paint brush in each cup.
3. Set the cups on a tray to take outdoors.
4. Put additional water in a pitcher.

ACTIVITY INTRODUCTION SUGGESTION:

"What do you use to write? Today we will write outside with water and brushes. What would you like to write?"

THEME INTRODUCTION SUGGESTION:

"Our unit is *community helpers*. Painters help make our community look good by keeping signs, homes, and businesses looking their best. Today we are going to go outside and pretend to be sign painters. Instead of using paint, we are going to use water. We will practice holding a paintbrush like a pencil and write like a sign painter. What would you like to write?"

continued

Outdoor Writing continued

PROCEDURES:

The children will complete the following steps:

1. Select a cup of water.

2. Hold the small paintbrush like a writing instrument to write with water on sidewalks, concrete, or buildings.

VARIATION:

Children may write in the sand box with craft sticks or on the concrete with chalk.

Portfolio of Stories

SKILL EXPLANATION:

Phonemic awareness is utilized as children sound out words that are unfamiliar to them. Knowledge of phonics assists the child in attempting to write words. Pairing reading and writing assists the child in fluency and comprehension.

ADULT PREPARATION:

1. Create an individual folder with each child's name.
2. Place the folders in a small box on the writing table.
3. Write the day's date on an index card and put it on the writing table.

ACTIVITY INTRODUCTION SUGGESTION:

"Today we are going to start our own folder of stories. Write your words on a piece of paper. Try to sound out words. If you prefer, you may draw a picture first and then write. Or you may draw a picture and then tell me what you'd like to write."

PROCEDURES:

The child will complete the following steps:

1. Write a story on plain paper.
2. Attempt to sound out words that are unfamiliar.
3. If unable to write, draw a picture; dictate to an adult what he or she would like to write as the adult writes the child's words directly on the paper.
4. Read what was written or listen to adult read what was dictated.
5. Write the date on the paper, with adult assistance if necessary.
6. Put the finished story page in his or her folder.

The adult will complete the following steps:

1. Arrange each child's papers in chronological order.
2. Share the stories with parents at conference times to illustrate how the child is progressing.
3. Give the child or parent the folder of stories at the close of the school year.

AGES: 4–6

GROUP SIZE:

2–4 children

DEVELOPMENTAL GOALS:

✂ To use words to create a story

✂ To develop writing skills

LEARNING OBJECTIVE:

Using a folder, index card, plain paper, and pencils or colored pencils, the child will create a story.

MATERIALS:

File folders
Small box
Permanent marker
Index cards
Plain paper
Pencil or colored pencils

continued

Portfolio of Stories continued

NOTE:

- ✄ If children are unable to write the date, the adult may write it on the papers before they set them on the table.

- ✄ To assist children in finding their own folder, use different colors of folders, add the child's photo, or put a different sticker after each name (e.g., a dinosaur sticker after one name, a butterfly sticker after another).

Predicting an Outcome

GROUP SIZE:
6–20 children

DEVELOPMENTAL GOALS:
✂ To develop listening skills
✂ To enhance cognitive development through prediction

LEARNING OBJECTIVE:
Using a book, chart tablet or large sheet of paper, and a marker, the children will listen to a story and predict the outcome.

MATERIALS:
Book
Chart tablet or large sheet of paper
Permanent marker

SKILL EXPLANATION:
An appreciation of literacy and print awareness are developed as children listen to a story and watch as the adult writes down predictions.

ADULT PREPARATION:
1. Select a book to read to the children.

ACTIVITY INTRODUCTION SUGGESTION:
"Today we are going to read a story. We will stop before the end and write down what you think will happen."

THEME INTRODUCTION SUGGESTION:
"Our unit is *flowers*. We're going to read the *Tulips* by Jay O'Callahan. We will stop before the end and write down what you think will happen."

continued

Predicting an Outcome continued

NOTE:

This activity would fit any theme depending upon the book chosen.

PROCEDURES:

The children will complete the following steps:

1. Listen to an adult read a storybook. The adult will stop before the story is finished and ask, "What do you think will happen next?"
2. Take turns answering the question as the adult writes the answers on a large sheet of paper.
3. Listen to the adult read all the answers.
4. Listen to the rest of the book.

BOOK SUGGESTIONS:

✂ Read *Tulips* by Jay O'Callahan, illustrated by Debrah Santini. (Atlanta, GA: Peachtree Publishers, 1992). A mischievous boy always plays tricks on his grandmother and her servants. His most grand prank involves Grandmother's precious tulips. Ask the children, "What will happen when the tulips come up?"

✂ Read *Popcorn* by Frank Asch. (New York: Parent's Magazine Press, 1979). Sam Bear stayed home alone while his parents went to a Halloween party. Sam's friends came over and they made so much popcorn it filled the house! Ask the children, "How will Sam and his friends clean the house?"

Queen's Crown

SKILL EXPLANATION:

An appreciation of literacy is enhanced through the development of listening skills. The use of rhyming words aids the development of phonemic awareness as the children listen and say the similar ending sounds. Fluency is improved through the recognition and use of color words.

ADULT PREPARATION:

1. Write the words to *Queen's Crown* on a poster board with a permanent marker; leave room to glue the crowns between each set of color sentences.

2. Make five copies of the crown pattern; color them brown, red, white, green, and blue.

3. Cut the crowns and use rubber cement to glue them above the appropriate color sentences.

ACTIVITY INTRODUCTION SUGGESTION:

"We are going to learn a new chant about a queen's crown. The problem is she has a different color crown for everything she does. You will need to listen and then repeat what I say."

THEME INTRODUCTION SUGGESTION:

"Our unit is *fairy tales*. What does a queen wear on her head? Today we are going to say a chant about a queen's crown."

PROCEDURES:

The children will complete the following steps:

1. Sit in a circle or semicircle.

2. Repeat the following chant while clapping once on each word:

   Adult: The Queen's crown is brown when she goes to town.

   Child: The Queen's crown is brown when she goes to town.

   Adult: The Queen's crown is red when she gets out of bed.

   Child: The Queen's crown is red when she gets out of bed.

   Adult: The Queen's crown is white when she flies a kite.

   Child: The Queen's crown is white when she flies a kite.

Sidebar

GROUP SIZE:
6–20 children

DEVELOPMENTAL GOALS:
- ✂ To develop listening skills
- ✂ To use rhyming words

LEARNING OBJECTIVE:
Using poster board with written words, the children will listen and repeat a chant.

MATERIALS:
Poster board
Permanent marker
Crown pattern (Appendix A28)
Crayons, markers, or colored pencils
Adult scissors
Rubber cement

continued

Q

Queen's Crown continued

Adult: The Queen's crown is green when she eats a string bean.

Child: The Queen's crown is green when she eats a string bean.

Adult: The Queen's crown is blue when she cries boo-hoo.

Child: The Queen's crown is blue when she cries boo-hoo.

BOOK SUGGESTION:

The Missing Tarts by B. G. Hennessy, illustrated by Tracey Campbell Pearson. (New York: Viking Penguin, Inc., 1989). Various Mother Goose characters help the Queen of Hearts seek out her missing tarts.

116

Quill Writing

SKILL EXPLANATION:

Writing letters as they are said increases the likelihood that alphabet recognition and fluency through word identification will be retained.

ADULT PREPARATION:

1. Copy the picture/word cards (Appendix B6) on card stock paper.
2. Cut the cards apart.
3. Laminate the picture/word cards, or cover them with clear contact paper.
4. Place the picture/word cards in a small basket.
5. Cover the table with newspaper.
6. Put different colors of diluted tempera paint in small plastic cups.
7. Place a quill beside each cup of paint on the table.

ACTIVITY INTRODUCTION SUGGESTION:

"What words can you think of that start with a *q*? Today we will write q words with a quill."

THEME INTRODUCTION SUGGESTION:

"Our unit is *communication*. Many, many years ago, people didn't have computers to write with. They wrote letters to each other. They didn't even have pens or pencils! They wrote with a feathered quill and a little ink pot."

PROCEDURES:

The child will complete the following steps:

1. Put on a smock.
2. Select a picture/word card from the basket.
3. Spell each letter in the word in a left-to-right progression.
4. Say the word out loud. Look at the picture for a hint.
5. Dip the quill in the paint.
6. Write each letter in the word, dipping the quill in the paint as needed.
7. Replace the picture/word card in the basket.
8. Repeat steps 2–6 with other picture/word cards.

AGES: 4–6

GROUP SIZE:
4–6 children

DEVELOPMENTAL GOALS:
- ✂ To develop writing skills
- ✂ To recognize alphabet letters and words

LEARNING OBJECTIVES:
Using a quill and tempera paint, the child will write words.

MATERIALS:
Picture/word cards (Appendix B6)
Card stock paper
Scissors
Laminator or clear contact paper
Small basket
Newspaper
Tempera paint (assorted colors)
Small plastic cups
Quills
Smocks

Q

AGES: 4–6

GROUP SIZE:

2–4 children

DEVELOPMENTAL GOALS:

✂ To identify words

✂ To develop writing skills

LEARNING OBJECTIVE:

Using index cards and yarn, the child will identify and write selected words.

MATERIALS:

Permanent marker
Index cards
Hole punch
Yarn
Adult scissors
Paper
Markers or crayons

Quilt of Words

SKILL EXPLANATION:

Fluency is enhanced through the recognition of words. Retention of the words is more easily achieved when paired with writing.

ADULT PREPARATION:

1. Write words children are to learn on index cards.
2. Punch holes around the edges of the index cards.
3. To create a quilt, weave the words together by stringing yarn through the holes.
4. Punch holes through additional index cards making enough for each child to have the number of cards equal to the number of words on the quilt.
5. Hang the quilt on the wall.
6. Write the words on a sheet of paper and place it at the writing table.

ACTIVITY INTRODUCTION SUGGESTION:

"We are going to make a special quilt. What is a quilt? It is a blanket that is made by sewing smaller pieces together. Our quilt will be made of words."

continued

Quilt of Words continued

THEME INTRODUCTION SUGGESTION:

"Our unit is *family*. Many families have quilts that they have made. Today we will make a quilt of words."

PROCEDURES:

The child will complete the following steps:

1. Identify the words on the class quilt hanging on the wall.

2. Copy the words on individual index cards, with a marker or crayon, while looking at the words at the writing table.

3. Weave the words together with yarn. Go in and out of the punched holes with the yarn to create a quilt.

4. Tie a knot, with adult assistance if needed.

5. Take the quilt of words home.

6. As new words are learned, write them on index cards punched with holes.

7. Take the cards and a length of yarn home, to continue weaving the words together.

NOTE:

Younger children will need samples of the words to be written lying on the table. Young children find it easier to copy words when they are lying on the same plane. It is a more advanced skill to look at words on the wall and then copy them on the paper.

VARIATION:

Word cards taken home may be stapled together in book form.

BOOK SUGGESTIONS:

- ✂ *The Quiltmaker's Journey* by Jeff Brumbeau (New York: Orchard Books, 2004). In this tale, a rich, young woman discovers happiness in renouncing her wealth and giving of herself to those in need by making them beautiful quilts.

- ✂ *The Quilt Story* by Tony Johnston (New York: Putman, 1985). Two little girls, one from the past and the other from the present, are comforted by the same quilt when moving to a new house.

Rebus Books

GROUP SIZE:

2–6 children

DEVELOPMENTAL GOALS:

✂ To identify words

✂ To understand sentences are made of words

LEARNING OBJECTIVE:

Using pictures of children, glue, and sentences, the children will create and read a rebus book.

MATERIALS:

Permission form to be photographed and videotaped (Appendix B3)

Digital camera or camera and film

Pictures of children

Pictures of objects

Copy paper

Adult scissors

Ruler

Rebus page (Appendix B7)

SKILL EXPLANATION:

Print awareness is developed as children understand that the symbols represent words. Fluency is promoted through the recognition of frequently used words.

ADULT PREPARATION:

1. Make sure there is a copy of the permission form on file for each child to be photographed (Appendix B3).
2. Take pictures of the children and familiar objects around the classroom or at home.
3. Make five copies of the child's face and one copy of four objects for each child.
4. Cut out the faces of the children and the objects into 1″ squares.
5. Place the faces in one stack on the table. Place the objects into a different stack.
6. Copy Appendix B7 with the following lines; glue on a sheet of construction paper with rubber cement.

   a. ■ sat on the □.

   b. ■ is on the □.

   c. ■ is in the □.

   d. ■ has a □.

   e. Where is ■?

ACTIVITY INTRODUCTION SUGGESTION:

"We will make a special book. It has words and pictures we will glue into sentences."

THEME INTRODUCTION SUGGESTION:

"Our unit is *my school*. We are going to make a book whose sentences have both pictures and words. The pictures will be of people in our class."

continued

Rebus Books continued

PROCEDURES:

The children will complete the following steps:

1. Glue the face of a child over the ■.
2. Glue a picture on an object over the □.
3. Read the sentences, inserting the child's name and the object's name.

The adult will complete the following steps:

1. Write *Where Are We?* on a sheet of blank paper to create a cover page.
2. When the glue is dry, laminate the pages, or cover them with clear contact paper.
3. Bind the pages into a book by punching holes on the left side of the page and attaching them using metal rings.
4. Read the book to the class and then set it in the book corner for children to read.

BOOK SUGGESTIONS:

✄ *Our Class Took a Trip to the Zoo* by Shirley Neitzel (New York: Greenwillow Books, 2002). A boy loses items throughout the zoo in this rebus book told in the format of "This is the house that Jack built."

✄ *Inside a Barn in the Country* by Alyssa Satin Capucilli (New York: Scholastic, 1995). Children will enjoy helping make the animal sound words in this rebus book.

MATERIALS:

Construction paper
Rubber cement
White school glue
Permanent marker
Laminator or clear contact paper
Hole punch
2" Metal rings

Record Writing

AGES: 3–6

DEVELOPMENTAL GOALS:

✂ To develop pre-writing skills

✂ To strengthen eye-hand coordination

LEARNING OBJECTIVES:

Using a marker, record player, and paper plate, the child will hold a marker correctly while creating a design.

MATERIALS:

Pen
Paper plate
Masking tape
Record player
Optional: Vinyl record

SKILL EXPLANATION:

Holding a marker in a writing position will help the child develop pre-writing skills. Writing will later aid the development of reading as the two develop jointly.

ADULT PREPARATION:

1. Use the pen to poke a hole in the center of the paper plate.
2. Secure the needle by taping the arm of the record player in the resting position.
3. Plug the record player into an outlet.
4. Place a paper plate on the turntable as though it were a record.

ACTIVITY INTRODUCTION SUGGESTION:

"What do you usually put on a record player? We put a plate on the player that we will use to write."

THEME INTRODUCTION SUGGESTION:

"Our unit is *music*. This is a record player. In the past, people did not have CDs. They listened to music on a record." [Optional: Show the children a vinyl record.]

continued

Record Writing continued

PROCEDURES:

The child will complete the following steps:

1. Watch the adult turn the record player on.
2. Take the cap off a marker.
3. Hold a marker in the writing position.
4. Hold the marker on the plate.
5. Watch as the plate turns and the marker makes circles on the plate.
6. Repeat steps 2–5 using different colors of markers.

NOTE:

Children often mistake the vinyl record for a black CD. Take the opportunity to play the record so the children can hear the music.

SAFETY PRECAUTIONS:

✂ Avoid giving children under the age of three a marker with a cap. Caps may be a choking hazard. Instead, remove the caps and place the markers in a bowl.

✂ The cord may be taped to the floor to prevent children from tripping over the cord.

Shaving Cream Writing

AGES: 3–6

GROUP SIZE:

2–4 children

DEVELOPMENTAL GOALS:

- ✄ To recognize sight words
- ✄ To strengthen writing skills

LEARNING OBJECTIVES:

Using shaving cream and word cards, the child will write sight words.

MATERIALS:

Dolch words (Appendix B1)
Index cards
Fine-tipped marker
Shaving cream or tray
Table

SKILL EXPLANATION:

Writing and reading compliment each other as children recognize sight words, which advances the skill of fluency.

ADULT PREPARATION:

1. Select words from Appendix B1 to write on index cards with a fine-tipped marker.
2. Spread a thin layer of shaving cream on a clean table or tray.
3. Set the cards in a plastic basket on the table.

ACTIVITY INTRODUCTION SUGGESTION:

"What do people do with shaving cream? Today we will write with shaving cream."

THEME INTRODUCTION SUGGESTION:

"Our theme is *family*. In your family, who uses shaving cream? Today we will do something different with shaving cream. We will write with shaving cream."

continued

Shaving Cream Writing continued

PROCEDURES:

1. Put on a smock.
2. Select a word from the basket.
3. Identify the letters in the word.
4. Identify the word, with adult help if necessary.
5. Using an index finger, write the word in the shaving cream.
6. Wipe hands with a paper towel.
7. Put the word card back in the basket.
8. Select another word card.
9. Repeat steps 2–7.

NOTE:

The word cards may be laminated or covered with clear contact paper for extended use.

SAFETY PRECAUTION:

Use non-menthol shaving cream.

Sign-in Board

AGES: 4–6

GROUP SIZE:

1–2 children

DEVELOPMENTAL GOALS:

✂ To develop writing skills

✂ To develop a sense of responsibility

LEARNING OBJECTIVE:

Using a clipboard or folder, copy paper, and a washable marker, the children will write their names when entering the room.

MATERIALS:

Clipboard or folder
Copy paper
Washable marker

SKILL EXPLANATION:

Fluency will develop as children learn to practice writing their names. As the year progresses, they will also recognize the names of their classmates.

ADULT PREPARATION:

1. Place paper on the clipboard.
2. Write numbers 1 to the number of children in the class.
3. Place the clipboard and marker on a table near the door.

ACTIVITY INTRODUCTION SUGGESTION:

Show the children the clipboard and say, "Each day when you come in, this clipboard will be sitting here. Choose a marker and write your name on the clipboard."

PROCEDURES:

The children will complete the following step:

1. Upon arrival, use the marker to write their name after a number.

NOTE:

As the year progresses, the handwriting will improve.

VARIATIONS:

✂ Write the children's first name on a cutout, and place the cutouts on a table. When the children arrive, they find their name, and then put their cutout in a basket, or pocket folder.

✂ Mid-year, change to last names.

126

Song Board Singing

SKILL EXPLANATION:

Print awareness is developed as children sing the words written on a song board.

ADULT PREPARATION:

1. Write the words to *Singing and Reading* on a poster board.
2. Copy and paste music notes on the poster board with rubber cement.

ACTIVITY INTRODUCTION SUGGESTION:

"We are going to learn a new song about reading. Our song is written on this board. I will point to the words as we sing."

THEME INTRODUCTION SUGGESTION:

"Our unit is *books*. Some books have songs to sing along with."

PROCEDURES:

The children will complete the following steps:

1. Look at the song board as the adult touches each word as it is sung.
2. Sing the following song to the tune of *Mary had a Little Lamb*:

Singing and Reading

Reading is the thing to do, thing to do, thing to do,

Reading is the thing to do, it makes my heart sing.

Singing is the thing to do, thing to do, thing to do,

Singing is the thing to do; it helps my brain to grow.

NOTE:

Music utilizes both sides of the brain, which facilitates learning.

BOOK SUGGESTIONS:

- ✂ *Bingo* by Rosemary Wells (New York: Scholastic Press, 1999). This brief board book follows the words to the song, *Bingo*.
- ✂ *Today is Monday* by Eric Carle. (New York: Scholastic, Inc., 1993). The days of the week are introduced with food. This book includes the music to sing with the text.

AGES: 3–6

GROUP SIZE:

4–20 children

DEVELOPMENTAL GOALS:

- ✂ To associate words with corresponding print
- ✂ To promote oral expression

LEARNING OBJECTIVE:

The children will participate in reading and singing from a song board.

MATERIALS:

Poster board
Marker
Music note pattern (Appendix A29)
Rubber cement

Stamp Name Game

AGES: 3–6

GROUP SIZE:

2–6 children

DEVELOPMENTAL GOALS:

✂ To recognize their name

✂ To identify alphabet letters

LEARNING OBJECTIVE:

Using an index card and stamps, the children will identify the letters in their name.

MATERIALS:

Permanent marker
Index cards
Tag board
Adult scissors
Basket
Smocks
Alphabet stamps
Washable stamp pad

SKILL EXPLANATION:

Print awareness is developed as children recognize the letters of their names. Fluency is enhanced when the children put the letters in proper order to spell and recognize their names.

ADULT PREPARATION:

1. Write each child's name at the top of individual index cards. Space the letters apart to equal the width of the letter stamps.

2. Write lowercase alphabet letters on tag board. Cut the letters apart and put them in a basket.

3. Put the name cards, basket of letters, alphabet stamps, and washable stamp pad on the table.

continued

128

Stamp Name Game continued

ACTIVITY INTRODUCTION SUGGESTION:

"Our names are made up of letters. We are going to spell our names using alphabet stamps."

THEME INTRODUCTION SUGGESTION:

"Our unit is *all about me*. You will spell your name with letter stamps."

PROCEDURES:

The children will complete the following steps:

1. Put on smock.
2. Find the index card with their name.
3. Pull a letter from the basket. Identify the letter, with adult help if needed.
4. If their name has that letter, use that letter stamp to stamp the letter under the same letter in their name on the index card.
5. Repeat steps 3–4 until all names have been spelled out with stamps.

VARIATION:

In place of writing letters on paper, use magnetic or plastic letters.

Toast Writing

GROUP SIZE:

3–6 children

DEVELOPMENTAL GOALS:

✂ To develop print awareness

✂ To enhance fluency

LEARNING OBJECTIVES:

Using a rebus recipe and ingredients, the children will read the chart and write on bread.

MATERIALS:

Copy paper
Rebus recipe for toast writing (Appendix D4)
New, never used, narrow paint brushes
Baking sheet
Aluminum foil
Sliced bread
Paper plates
Smocks
¼ cup measure
Milk
Bowls
Food coloring
Spoons
Fine-tipped permanent marker

SKILL EXPLANATION:

Print awareness is developed as children realize they are responsible for the marks made as they write on the toast. It is also expanded by the realization that the symbols on the rebus recipe represent words. Fluency is encouraged by the reading of the simple words on the rebus recipe.

ADULT PREPARATION:

1. Copy the rebus recipe for toast writing (Appendix D4).
2. Wash new, never used, narrow paint brushes in a dishwasher or with hot, soapy water.
3. Wash hands and wash the table.
4. Cover a baking sheet with aluminum foil.
5. Set a slice of bread on individual paper plates.
6. Place the rebus recipe and the ingredients on the clean table.
7. Preheat the oven to broil.

continued

Toast Writing continued

ACTIVITY INTRODUCTION SUGGESTION:

"Where do you usually write? Today we will write on bread with colored milk."

THEME INTRODUCTION SUGGESTION:

"Our theme is *colors*. What color is the bread you eat? Today we will write on bread with different colors of milk."

PROCEDURES:

The children will complete the following steps:

1. Read the rebus recipe, with adult help if needed.
2. Wash hands.
3. Put on a smock.
4. Measure ¼ cup milk into a bowl.
5. Place several drops of food coloring into the bowl.
6. Stir the mixture with a spoon.
7. Select a paper plate with a slice of bread.
8. Use the narrow brush to write with colored milk on the piece of bread.
9. Use separate brushes for each color of milk.
10. When finished, set the piece of bread with milk writing on the foil-covered baking sheet.
11. Write their name below the bread on the foil with a permanent marker.

The adult will complete the following steps:

1. Once the baking sheet is full, broil the bread until the milk on the toast is dry or the unwritten parts are golden brown. This will take approximately 5 minutes.
2. Set each piece of toast on a paper plate. Write each child's name on the plate with his or her toast.
3. Set the toast out for snack.

Tracing Letters

AGES: 3½–6

GROUP SIZE:

2–4 children

DEVELOPMENTAL GOALS:

- ✂ To develop writing skills
- ✂ To hold a writing instrument correctly

LEARNING OBJECTIVE:

Using construction paper and markers or crayons, the child will hold a writing instrument correctly as they trace alphabet letters.

MATERIALS:

9" × 12" sheets of light colored construction paper
Permanent marker
White school glue
Water-based marker or crayons

SKILL EXPLANATION:

Print awareness is developed through the recognition of alphabet letters. Identification of the letters is enhanced through the association of writing the letters.

ADULT PREPARATION:

1. Fold a sheet of 9" × 12" construction paper into thirds; make one for each child.
2. Lay the paper flat and on the top third write selected alphabet letters with a permanent marker. Trace these letters with white school glue. Let dry.
3. On the middle third, write the same letters using broken lines. Write the letters in the same order as on top.
4. Leave the bottom third of the paper blank.

ACTIVITY INTRODUCTION SUGGESTION:

Show the children the letters made from glue and ask, "What are these letters? We are going to trace the letters with our finger, then connect the broken lines to form the letters."

THEME INTRODUCTION SUGGESTION:

"Our unit is *the five senses*. We will use one of our five senses to trace letters. What sense do we use to feel?"

PROCEDURES:

The child will complete the following steps:

1. Use his or her finger to trace the letters with raised glue; identify the letter as it is traced.
2. Hold a water-based marker or crayon correctly to trace over the letters made with broken lines.
3. Attempt to write the letters in the blank space.

Trademark Match

SKILL EXPLANATION:

Print awareness is developed through the understanding that symbols represent objects. Visual discrimination assists the child in finding matches that will later transfer to identifying the same words.

ADULT PREPARATION:

1. Cut trademark logos from magazines, newspapers, or cereal boxes. (Suggestions: McDonald's golden arches, the Kellogg's script from cereal boxes, Planters' Mr. Peanut, etc.)
2. Cut two of each trademark.
3. Use rubber cement to glue the trademarks on individual pieces of construction paper.
4. Lay one set on the table.
5. Place the identical set in a basket.

ACTIVITY INTRODUCTION SUGGESTION:

"We are going to play a matching game." Hold up each card and ask the child to identify each one. "These are trademarks. The trademark is a symbol for that company's name."

THEME INTRODUCTION SUGGESTION:

"Our unit is *food*." Show one card from each pair. "What is on these cards? These are companies' trademarks. The trademark is a symbol for the company. These companies make food."

PROCEDURES:

The child will complete the following steps:
1. Identify the trademark on the table, with adult help if necessary.
2. Select and identify a trademark from the basket.
3. Place the selected trademark with the identical one on the table.
4. Repeat steps 2–3 until all trademarks have been matched.

GROUP SIZE:

2–4 children

DEVELOPMENTAL GOALS:

✄ To enhance print awareness
✄ To develop visual discrimination

LEARNING OBJECTIVE:

Using trademarks or logos, the child will find identical pairs.

MATERIALS:

Magazines, newspapers, or cereal boxes
Adult scissors
Construction paper
Rubber cement
Basket

continued

Trademark Match continued

NOTE:

Glue matching trademarks on the same color of construction paper to assist younger children in matching.

BOOK SUGGESTION:

I Read Signs by Tana Hoban (New York: Greenwillow Books, 1983). Familiar signs are photographed that children may recognize and read.

Traveling Pet

SKILL EXPLANATION:

Print awareness is developed through writing or watching an adult write what the child dictates. An appreciation of literacy is enhanced as the journals are read to the class.

ADULT PREPARATION:

1. Select a stuffed animal to be the class pet.
2. Place a small suitcase or book bag and the pet's blanket and toys on the table.
3. Choose a name for the pet; write the pet's name on a journal (e.g., *Rover's Amazing Journeys*).
4. Copy family letter (Appendix B8) and fill in the date and the pet's name.

ACTIVITY INTRODUCTION SUGGESTION:

"What kind of care does a pet need? Each week we will take turns taking home our special class pet. He is not a real pet; however, I want you to pretend he is and take care of him just as you would a real pet. He is going to bring a special notebook. Either you or someone in your family may write down everything you do with our pet. Bring every-thing back on Monday and you'll be able to tell us what you and our pet did together."

continued

AGES: 5–6

GROUP SIZE:
1 child

DEVELOPMENTAL GOALS:

- ✂ To develop writing skills
- ✂ To promote oral expression

LEARNING OBJECTIVE:

Using a stuffed animal, suitcase or book bag, blanket, pet toys, journal, and marker, the child will write about their experiences and read them to the class.

MATERIALS:

Stuffed animal
Suitcase or book bag
Blanket
Pet toys
Journal
Marker
Family Letter 4
   (Appendix B8)

Traveling Pet continued

THEME INTRODUCTION SUGGESTION:

"Our unit is *pets*. Raise your hand if you have a pet at home. What kind of pet do you have? If you don't have a pet, what kind of pet would you like to have? What would you do to take care of a pet? Each week we will take turns taking home our special class pet."

PROCEDURES:

The child will complete the following steps:

1. Sign name to the bottom of the family letter.
2. Pack the pet's bag with his journal, blanket, and toys.
3. Take the pet home on the weekend.
4. Play with the pet and take him to the places the family visits.
5. With family's assistance, write in the journal what the pet does and where he goes. Older children may write their own entries. Younger children will need to dictate their story to a family member to write.
6. Return the journal, pet, and his toys to the classroom.
7. With adult assistance, read the journal to the class to tell them what the pet did over the weekend.

NOTE:

✀ Children will take turns taking the class pet home. One suggestion is to make a list and keep track of when each child takes it home. This will ensure all children have an equal number of turns.

✀ Stuffed animals or real class pets such as turtles or guinea pigs may be used.

BOOK SUGGESTIONS:

✀ *The Best Pet of All* by David LaRochelle (New York: Dutton Children's Books, 2004). A boy is unable to convince his mother to get a dog as a pet, until he brings home a dragon.

✀ *Pick a Pet* by Diane Namm (New York: Children's Press, 2004). A little girl tries to decide which pet to get. This easy reader has 44 words and only once sentence per page.

136

Umbrella Story Starter

AGES: 3–6

GROUP SIZE:
1 child

DEVELOPMENTAL GOALS:
- ✂ To associate words with written print
- ✂ To enhance oral expression

LEARNING OBJECTIVE:
Using an umbrella and pictures, the child will dictate a story.

MATERIALS:
Magazines, newspapers, or Internet
Adult scissors
Child-size umbrella
Masking tape
Unlined paper
Pencil, pen, or marker
Crayons

SKILL EXPLANATION:

An appreciation of literacy and print awareness are developed as children watch an adult write what they dictate and then listen to it being read.

ADULT PREPARATION:

1. Find rainy day pictures in magazines, newspapers, or on the Internet.
2. Cut the pictures out (or print them).
3. Open a child-size umbrella.
4. Tape one rainy day picture to each section of the umbrella.

ACTIVITY INTRODUCTION SUGGESTION:

"We have a special umbrella." Show the umbrella. "What do you see on the umbrella? What is in each picture?"

THEME INTRODUCTION SUGGESTION:

Show the umbrella. "Our unit is *weather*. In what kind of weather do you use an umbrella? This is a special indoor umbrella. What do you see on the umbrella? What is in each picture?"

continued

Umbrella Story Starter continued

PROCEDURES:

The child will complete the following steps:

1. Identify the pictures as he or she turns the umbrella.

2. Select one picture.

3. Dictate a story to the teacher about the selected picture.

The adult will complete the following steps:

1. Use unlined paper to write down what the child says regarding their picture.

2. When the child is finished, read the story back to the child.

The child will complete the following step:

1. Draw a picture under the written text.

VARIATIONS:

✂ Children cut their own pictures from magazines.

✂ Older children may not need to depend upon the adult to write for them. These children may select a picture and write their own story.

⚠ SAFETY PRECAUTION:

Make sure the child-size umbrella has bulbous safety tips on the spokes.

BOOK SUGGESTION:

The Umbrella by Jan Brett (New York: G. P. Putnam's Sons, 2004). A boy walks into a cloud forest with his umbrella, leaving it to search for animals. He doesn't see the myriad of animals that pile into his umbrella.

Under the Table Writing

AGES: 3–6

GROUP SIZE:
1–2 children

DEVELOPMENTAL GOALS:
- ✂ To develop print awareness
- ✂ To cultivate pre-writing skills

LEARNING OBJECTIVES:
Using paper taped under the table and markers, crayons, or colored pencils, the children will write while lying on their backs.

MATERIALS:
Masking tape
Paper
Blanket
Crayons, markers, and/ or colored pencils
Bowl

SKILL EXPLANATION:

Print awareness is developed as children realize they are responsible for the marks made on paper. This will expand to the recognition and writing of alphabet letters and words.

ADULT PREPARATION:

1. Tape a piece of paper on the underside of the table.
2. Lay a blanket on the floor under the table.
3. Set crayons, markers, or colored pencils in a bowl on the blanket.

ACTIVITY INTRODUCTION SUGGESTION:

"Michelangelo is an artist who lay on his back while he painted the ceiling of the Sistine chapel. Today we will lie on our backs while we write on the paper taped under the table."

THEME INTRODUCTION SUGGESTION:

"Our theme is *art*. Michelangelo is a great artist who lived a long time ago. One of the art works he is widely known for is painting the ceiling of the Sistine chapel. He did this by lying on his back on platforms that reached nearly to the ceiling. Today we will lie on our backs while we write on the paper taped under the table."

PROCEDURES:

The children will complete the following steps:

1. Lay on their backs on the blanket.
2. Set the bowl of crayons, markers, or colored pencils between them.
3. Lying on their backs, write on the paper.

NOTE:

If children have difficulty reaching the table while lying on their backs, put a tumbling mat, cot, or small mattress under the blanket.

VARIATION:

Names, words, or sentences may be taped under the table for the children to copy.

U

Underwater Letter Match

AGES: 3–6

GROUP SIZE:

2–4 children

DEVELOPMENTAL GOALS:

✄ To identify upper- and lowercase alphabet letters

✄ To enhance visual discrimination

LEARNING OBJECTIVE:

Using rocks and a plastic container with water, the children will match and identify alphabet letters.

MATERIALS:

Permanent marker
Rocks
Large plastic container
Water
Towel
Roll or stack of
    paper towels
Smocks

SKILL EXPLANATION:

Print awareness is developed through the identification of alphabet letters. Visual discrimination assists children in telling the letters apart, which will transfer to the recognition of different letters and their sounds in words.

ADULT PREPARATION:

1. Write identical alphabet letters on two sets of rocks with a permanent marker.

2. Fill a plastic container half full of water.

continued

Underwater Letter Match continued

3. Set the rocks on the bottom of the container. Turn the rocks so the letter is not visible.

4. Lay a small towel on the table.

5. Place a roll or stack of paper towel on the table.

ACTIVITY INTRODUCTION SUGGESTION:

"Lakes, rivers, and oceans often have rocks underneath their surface." Show the tub of water on the table and say, "In our water we have rocks; there are alphabet letters written on our rocks. We want to find the rocks with the same alphabet letters."

THEME INTRODUCTION SUGGESTION:

"Our unit is *ocean*. Sometimes divers look for treasures under the sea. In some parts there are rocks on the ocean floor. This tub is our pretend ocean. The treasure in our ocean is matching rocks. We want to find rocks with the same alphabet letter on them."

PROCEDURES:

The children will take turns to complete the following steps:

1. Put on a smock and roll up sleeves if necessary.

2. Reach underwater and turn over two rocks.

3. Identify the letters on each rock.

4. If the rocks have the same letter, remove them from the water and place them on the towel.

5. If the rocks have different letters, turn the rocks over again so the letter isn't visible.

6. Repeat steps 2–5 until all rocks have been removed from the water.

7. Dry hands with a paper towel and throw it away.

NOTE:

Start with 6–8 matches. Increase as the child's skill level and attention span increases.

 ## SAFETY PRECAUTION:

Use rocks that are large enough to prevent a choking hazard.

Vehicle Word Match

AGES: 3–6

GROUP SIZE:

2–4 children

DEVELOPMENTAL GOALS:

✂ To develop visual discrimination

✂ To classify objects through matching

LEARNING OBJECTIVE:

Using vehicle cutouts, the child will match identical items.

MATERIALS:

Vehicle patterns (Appendix 21, 30–33)
   Car (Appendix 21)
   Truck (Appendix 30)
   Van (Appendix 31)
   Bus (Appendix 32)
   Jeep (Appendix 33)
Markers, crayons, or colored pencils
Adult scissors

SKILL EXPLANATION:

Visual discrimination assists the child in matching identical items. This will transfer to the discrimination of word identification.

ADULT PREPARATION:

1. Make an even number of copies of each vehicle pattern.
2. Cut out the vehicles. Color two of each identical vehicle the same, (i.e., cut out four jeeps, color two jeeps green and two jeeps blue).
3. Separate the identical vehicles into two stacks.

ACTIVITY INTRODUCTION SUGGESTION:

"At times when I'm driving, I'll see another van just like mine. It will be the same colors and shape as mine. Today we are going to find the matches for all these vehicles."

THEME INTRODUCTION SUGGESTION:

"Our unit is *transportation*. Transportation is the way we move people or things from one place to another. We often transport things in vehicles. What are the vehicles on the table?"

PROCEDURES:

The child will complete the following steps:

1. Lay one stack of vehicles in a row on the table.
2. Look at the other stack of vehicles. Select the top vehicle from this stack.
3. Note the details of the vehicle, answering questions such as "How many doors does it have?" and "What color is it?"
4. Lay it with the identical vehicle on the table.
5. Repeat steps 2–4 until all vehicles have been matched.

VARIATION:

Write the name of the vehicle on each cutout (i.e., write *van* on each van, *car* on each car, etc.). Children may identify and match the vehicle words.

BOOK SUGGESTION:

The Little Auto by Lois Lenski (New York: Random House, 1962). Mr. Small takes care of his car.

Vocabulary Building Blocks

AGES: 5–6

GROUP SIZE:
2–4 children

DEVELOPMENTAL GOALS:
- ✂ To identify words
- ✂ To coordinate large and small muscles

LEARNING OBJECTIVE:
Using word blocks, the children will coordinate muscles to build structures with the identified words.

MATERIALS:
Adult scissors
Construction paper
Blocks
Dolch words
   (Appendix B1)
Masking tape

SKILL EXPLANATION:
Fluency will be developed as children identify words. Retention of the words will be stimulated by the coordination of muscle use.

ADULT PREPARATION:
1. Cut construction paper into rectangles or squares to fit the blocks.
2. Select words from Appendix B1 to write on the construction paper.
3. Tape each word to a block. Use only one side of each block.

continued

Vocabulary Building Blocks continued

ACTIVITY INTRODUCTION SUGGESTION:

"We are going to build with blocks. There are words on our blocks. Say the word written on the block. If you know the word, set that block to the side. You will be able to build with the word blocks you know."

THEME INTRODUCTION SUGGESTION:

"Our unit is *community helpers*. Some community helpers work in construction; they help build things. Today we are going to build with word blocks. We will build with the blocks whose words we know."

PROCEDURES:

The children will take turns to complete the following steps:

1. Identify the words on the blocks.
2. Use words correctly identified to build a structure together.
3. Set incorrectly identified words to the side until they are correctly identified.

NOTE:

Cans, milk cartons, shoe boxes, or other items may be used in place of blocks.

VARIATION:

Create a mobile with identified words by hanging word cards with yarn from a hanger.

BOOK SUGGESTION:

Raise the Roof! by Anastasia Suen (New York: Viking, 2003). Cartoon-like illustrations and simple text show a house being built.

Vowel Song

SKILL EXPLANATION:

Through the identification of the initial sound in a word, phonemic awareness is enhanced.

ADULT PREPARATION:

1. Copy and color the vowel picture cards.

ACTIVITY INTRODUCTION SUGGESTION:

"We are going to sing a new song using our vowels. The vowels are *a, e, i, o,* and *u.* The vowels are alphabet letters that have two sounds." Show each picture card and ask the children to identify the object in the picture. Stress the beginning sound in each picture.

THEME INTRODUCTION SUGGESTION:

"Our unit is *music.* We can make music by playing an instrument or singing. Today we are going to sing a new song using vowels. The vowels are alphabet letters with two sounds. Let's look at the pictures with our vowel sounds."

PROCEDURES:

The children will complete the following step:

1. Sing the *Old McAlphabet Had a Vowel* song as the picture cards are held by the children.

> Old McAlphabet had a vowel,
> A E I O U

And in his apple he had a vowel, A a a a a	(*Child will hold the picture of an apple.*)
And in his gate he had a vowel. Ā ā ā ā ā	(*Child will hold the picture of a gate.*)
And in his egg he had a vowel. e e e e e	(*Child will hold the picture of an egg.*)
And in his bee he had a vowel. Ē ē ē ē ē	(*Child will hold the picture of a bee.*)
And in his iguana he had a vowel. I i i i i	(*Child will hold the picture of an iguana.*)

continued

AGES: 4–6

GROUP SIZE:
6–20 children

DEVELOPMENTAL GOALS:

- ✂ To develop phonemic awareness
- ✂ To recognize vowel sounds

LEARNING OBJECTIVE:

Using vowel picture cards, the children will sing a vowel song.

MATERIALS:

Copy paper
Crayons or colored pencils
Vowel picture cards (Appendix A7, A23, A34–A41)
Apple (Appendix A34)
Gate (Appendix A35)
Egg (Appendix A36)
Bee (Appendix A37)
Iguana (Appendix A38)
Kite (Appendix A23)
Ostrich (Appendix A39)
Goat (Appendix A7)
Sun (Appendix A40)
Mule (Appendix A41)

145

Vowel Song continued

And in his kite he had a vowel.
Ī ĭ ī ī ī

(Child will hold the picture of a kite.)

And in his ostrich he had a vowel.
O o o o o

(Child will hold the picture of an ostrich.)

And in his goat he had a vowel.
Ō ŏ ŏ ŏ ŏ

(Child will hold the picture of a goat.)

And in his sun he had a vowel.
U u u u u

(Child will hold the picture of a sun.)

And in his mule he had a vowel.
OO oo oo oo oo

(Child will hold the picture of a mule.)

Old McAlphabet had a vowel.
A E I O U

BOOK SUGGESTION:

Old MacDonald Had a Farm by Pam Addams (Auburn, ME: Child's Play, 2004). This book contains cutouts showing additional animals each time the page is turned.

Wild Thing Snack

AGES: 4–6

GROUP SIZE:
2–4 children

DEVELOPMENTAL GOALS:
- ✂ To improve listening skills
- ✂ To develop print awareness

LEARNING OBJECTIVE:
Using a book, rebus recipe, ingredients, and kitchen equipment, the children will make a snack.

MATERIALS:
Copy paper
Rebus recipe for wild thing snack (Appendix D5)
Book: *Where the Wild Things Are* by Maurice Sendak
Rice cakes
Paper plates
Plastic knives
Whipped cream cheese
Bowls
Cutting board
Paring knife
Grapes
Strawberries
Shredded cheese

SKILL EXPLANATION:

An appreciation of literacy is developed through listening to the adult read *Where the Wild Things Are*. Print awareness is encouraged by reading a rebus recipe and recognizing symbols represent words.

ADULT PREPARATION:

1. Duplicate rebus recipe (Appendix D5).
2. Wash hands.
3. Put a rice cake and plastic knife on individual paper plates.
4. Put whipped cream cheese in a bowl.
5. Use a cutting board and paring knife to cut grapes in half and slice strawberries; place each type of food in separate bowls.
6. Place shredded cheese in a bowl.

continued

Wild Thing Snack continued

ACTIVITY INTRODUCTION SUGGESTION:

"Today we will listen to *Where the Wild Things Are* by Maurice Sendak. After we read the book, we will read a recipe and make a wild thing snack."

THEME INTRODUCTION SUGGESTION:

"Our unit is *food*. What would a wild thing eat? We will listen to *Where the Wild Things Are* by Maurice Sendak, and then we will make a wild thing snack."

PROCEDURES:

The child will complete the following steps:

1. Listen to the adult read the book *Where the Wild Things Are* by Maurice Sendak.
2. Answer the question, "What features do all the wild things have in common?" [Hint: eyes, hair, mouth, teeth, claws]
3. Wash hands to make own wild things.

   a. Spread whipped cream cheese with a plastic knife.

   b. Add grapes for eyes.

   c. Add strawberries for mouth.

   d. Add cheese for hair and beards.

BOOK SUGGESTION:

Where the Wild Things Are by Maurice Sendak (New York: HarperCollins Children's Books, 1963).

Wordless Picture Books

SKILL EXPLANATION:

An appreciation of literacy is advanced through vocalizing a storyline in association with a wordless picture book.

ADULT PREPARATION:

1. Select wordless picture books for the children.

ACTIVITY INTRODUCTION SUGGESTION:

"We are going to look at a special book." Show the wordless book selected. Open the pages and flip through the book and ask, "What is missing from this book? When there are only pictures and no words, it is called a wordless picture book. In a book like this we will make up the story from the pictures."

THEME INTRODUCTION SUGGESTION:

"Our unit is *books*." Show the wordless book selected and ask, "What is the difference between this book and most books that we read? This book doesn't have any words. It is a wordless picture book."

PROCEDURES:

The children will take turns to complete the following steps:

1. Select a book.
2. Tell a story by looking at the pictures in the book.

BOOK SUGGESTIONS:

- ✂ *Tuesday* by David Wiesner (New York: Clarion Books, 1991). Frogs fly about town in this Caldecott Medal book.
- ✂ *Pancakes* by Tomie dePaola (New York: Scholastic, Inc., 1991). A woman makes pancakes from scratch. She even gathers eggs from the chickens and churns her own butter. Something happens to her pancakes, but she is able to solve the dilemma with the unwitting help of a neighbor.

continued

AGES: 3–5

GROUP SIZE:
2–4 children

DEVELOPMENTAL GOALS:
- ✂ To develop an appreciation of literacy
- ✂ To promote oral expression

LEARNING OBJECTIVE:
Using a wordless picture book, the children will tell a story from the visual examination of the pictures.

MATERIALS:
Wordless picture books

Wordless Picture Books continued

EXPANSION:

Allow each child to select a different book. Tape record the children as they "read." Put the book and the tape together at the listening center for other children to hear the story.

Worm Word Search

AGES: 4–6

GROUP SIZE:
2–4 children

DEVELOPMENTAL GOALS:
- ✄ To identify words
- ✄ To match words

LEARNING OBJECTIVE:
Using worm cutouts, sand, the sensory table or a large plastic container, and a sheet of words, the child will identify and match words.

MATERIALS:
Worm pattern (Appendix A42)
Copy paper
Colored pencils, crayons, or markers
Adult scissors
Fine-tipped permanent marker
Large sheet of construction paper
Laminator or clear contact paper
Sand
Large plastic container
Construction paper

SKILL EXPLANATION:
Fluency is increased as the child identifies words. It is further enhanced through matching identical words.

ADULT PREPARATION:
1. Copy, color, and cut multiple worm patterns.
2. Write selected words on the worms with a fine-tipped permanent marker.
3. Write the same words on a large sheet of construction paper and place them on the table.
4. Laminate the worms, or cover them with clear contact paper.
5. Put sand in the large plastic container.
6. Hide the worms in the sand.
7. Place the container of sand and worms on the table beside the sheet of construction paper with words.

ACTIVITY INTRODUCTION SUGGESTION:
"Today we are going on a worm search. Our worms have words written on them. We have the same words written on another piece of paper. When you find a worm, look at the word written on it and match it to the paper."

continued

Worm Word Search continued

THEME INTRODUCTION SUGGESTION:

"Our unit is *animals*. The worm is a long, thin animal without legs. The worm makes burrows in the ground. We will search for worm words in the sand."

PROCEDURES:

The child will complete the following steps:

1. Wash hands.
2. Search for a worm in the sand.
3. Identify the word on the worm, with adult assistance if needed.
4. Match and lay the worm word with the identical word on the construction paper.
5. Repeat steps 2–4 until all worms have been found and matched.

BOOK SUGGESTION:

Diary of a Worm by Doreen Cronin (New York: Scholastic, Inc., 2003). A young worm records his journal entries in a humorous look at his life.

X-Ray Vision

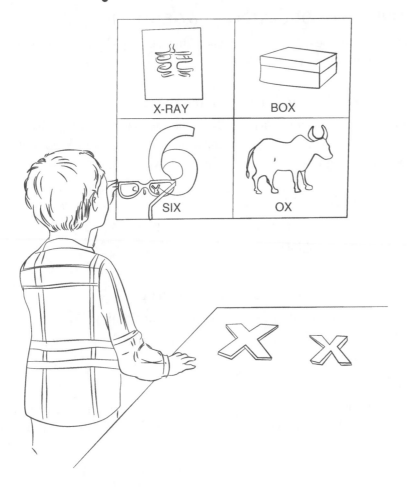

SKILL EXPLANATION:

Alphabet recognition is a prelude to reading. As the children couple this activity with the coordination of large and small muscles, retention of the alphabet names will be strengthened.

ADULT PREPARATION:

1. Remove lenses from plastic sunglasses.
2. Cut Xs out of foam sheets.
3. Hot glue the Xs on the front of each bow of the glasses.
4. Roll masking tape on the back of the foam Xs.
5. Stick the Xs around the room at the children's eye level.

continued

X

AGES: 3–5

GROUP SIZE:
2–4 children

DEVELOPMENTAL GOALS:
✂ To identify an alphabet letter
✂ To coordinate large and small muscles

LEARNING OBJECTIVE:
Using the frames from a pair of plastic sunglasses and foam Xs, the children will search, pick up, and identify the letter X.

MATERIALS:
Plastic sunglasses
Foam sheets
Adult scissors
Hot glue gun
Hot glue gun sticks
Masking tape
Large sheet of paper
Permanent marker
"X" items or pictures (box, exercise, exit, fax, lox, mix, ox, six, saxophone, x-ray, and xylophone)

X-Ray Vision continued

ACTIVITY INTRODUCTION SUGGESTION:

Show the glasses. "What letter is on these glasses? We are going to use these special glasses to look for the letter X hidden in the room."

THEME INTRODUCTION SUGGESTION:

"Our unit is *community helpers*. Some people have the job of taking X-rays of our bones using a special machine. Today we are going to use special X-ray glasses to look for the letter X."

PROCEDURES:

The children will complete the following steps:

1. Put on X-ray glasses.
2. Search for Xs around the room.
3. When an X is found, stick the X to clothing.
4. Make the sound of X as it is placed on the clothing.
5. With adult assistance, make a list of the words containing an *x*.

NOTE:

Suggestions of "X" words include box, exercise, exit, fax, lox, mix, ox, six, saxophone, X-ray, or xylophone. If possible, show the items or pictures of them as they are listed.

154

Xylophone Letter Match

GROUP SIZE:
2 children

DEVELOPMENTAL GOALS:
✄ To identify alphabet letters
✄ To match alphabet letters

LEARNING OBJECTIVE:
Using rectangles and a xylophone, child will identify and match alphabet letters.

MATERIALS:
Construction paper
Pencil
Toy xylophone with letters written on keys
Adult scissors
Marker
Self-sticking magnetic tape
Mallet for xylophone

SKILL EXPLANATION:

When identifying and matching alphabet letters is paired with sensory stimulation and muscle movement, there is a greater likelihood for retention.

ADULT PREPARATION:

1. Using construction paper, trace and cut the size of each key on a xylophone, creating rectangles.

2. Note the letter on each key (c, d, e, f, g, a, b, c). This is an octave of music, which includes the eight notes of a scale. Each letter is a note. Write the letter on the same size of construction paper rectangle.

3. Cut, peel, and stick a section of magnetic tape on the back of each rectangle.

continued

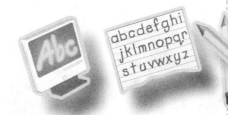

Xylophone Letter Match continued

ACTIVITY INTRODUCTION SUGGESTION:

Hold up the xylophone and say, "This is a xylophone. Listen to the sound it makes." Hit each key with the mallet. "Each key makes a different sound. Each key is a special note. The name of the key is written on it. It is an alphabet letter. What is the name of each key?"

THEME INTRODUCTION SUGGESTION:

"Our unit is *music*. We can make music with a xylophone. We use this xylophone to match alphabet letters."

PROCEDURES:

The child will complete the following steps:

1. Use the mallet to tap the xylophone key as he or she identifies the letter on the key.
2. Find the same letter on a rectangle.
3. Place magnetic alphabet piece on the corresponding xylophone key.
4. Repeat steps 1–3 matching all alphabet letters and rectangles.

NOTE:

If the letters are the same, the rectangle will be the same size as the key on the xylophone.

Yarn Words

AGES: 3–5

GROUP SIZE:
2–6 children

DEVELOPMENTAL GOALS:
✂ To identify words
✂ To develop pre-writing skills

LEARNING OBJECTIVE:
Using tag board, a cotton swab, glue, and yarn, the child will identify and trace words.

MATERIALS:
Adult scissors
Tag board
Ruler
Pencil
Yarn
White school glue
Milk caps
Cotton swabs

SKILL EXPLANATION:

Fluency is expanded with the identification of words. Tracing the words with cotton swabs and glue is an act of pre-writing. The ability to write accompanies the ability to read.

ADULT PREPARATION:

1. Cut tag board into 4" × 12" strips.
2. Use a pencil to write a selected word on each strip.
3. Cut yarn into 1" lengths.
4. Put glue in milk caps.

ACTIVITY INTRODUCTION SUGGESTION:

"Every word is made up of letters. We are going to name the words and letters on each card. We are going to cover the letters with yarn."

THEME INTRODUCTION SUGGESTION:

"Our unit is *the five senses*. Today we are going to use our sense of touch to write out a word."

continued

Yarn Words continued

PROCEDURES:

The child will complete the following steps:

1. Select a strip of tag board with a written word.

2. Identify the word, with adult assistance if needed.

3. Identify each letter in the word.

4. Use a cotton swab to trace the first letter in the word with glue.

5. Lay the short lengths of yarn on the glue to form the letter, saying the letter name out loud.

6. Repeat steps 4–5 until all letters have been outlined with yarn.

7. Identify the word again.

8. Once the glue is dry, trace the yarn letters with a finger, identifying each letter and identifying the word.

Yeniel the Yak

SKILL EXPLANATION:

An appreciation of literacy and print awareness are cultivated through listening and repeating what is written on the song board. Through alliteration, children will also develop phonemic awareness by listening to and repeating sounds.

ADULT PREPARATION:

1. Create a song board by writing *Yeniel the Yak* on poster board.
2. Copy, color, and cut the yak pattern.
3. Use rubber cement to glue the yak on the song board.

ACTIVITY INTRODUCTION SUGGESTION:

"We are going to sing an echo song about Yeniel the Yak. In an echo song, you will put on your good listening ears and listen to a part of the song being sung, and then you echo it back."

THEME INTRODUCTION SUGGESTION:

"Our unit is *animals*. What animal starts with the letter *y*? A yak starts with a *y*. Today we are going to sing a song about an animal named Yeniel, who happens to be a yak."

PROCEDURES:

The children will complete the following steps:

1. Listen to the adult make the *y* sound.
2. Repeat the *y* sound.
3. Chant *Yeniel the Yak* as an echo after the adult:

> Adult: Yeniel the yak cannot yodel.
> Child: Yeniel the yak cannot yodel.
> Adult: Yeniel the yak yells, "Yellow!"
> Child: Yeniel the yak yells, "Yellow!"
> Adult: Yeniel the yak should yodel,
> Child: Yeniel the yak should yodel,
> Adult: You-hoo, you-hoo, you-hoo.
> Child: You-hoo, you-hoo, you-hoo.

continued

AGES: 3–5

GROUP SIZE:
6–20 children

DEVELOPMENTAL GOALS:

- ✂ To develop listening skills
- ✂ To practice alliteration

LEARNING OBJECTIVE:

Using a song board, the children will listen and repeat an alliteration chant.

MATERIALS:

Poster board
Permanent marker
Yak pattern
   (Appendix 43)
Copy paper
Colored pencils or
   crayons
Adult scissors
Rubber cement

Yeniel the Yak continued

BOOK SUGGESTION:

Go Track a Yak by Tony Johnston (New York: Simon & Schuster Books for Young Readers, 2003). Following the advice of a witch, Papa tracks a yak to get "yak juice" for his hungry baby.

Zipper Bag Story

AGES: 3–6

GROUP SIZE:
2–4 children

DEVELOPMENTAL GOALS:
✄ To promote oral expression
✄ To develop an appreciation of literacy

LEARNING OBJECTIVE:
Using a zipper bag book of pictures, the child will identify the people and activities and tell a story.

MATERIALS:
Permission form to be photographed and videotaped (Appendix B3)
Digital camera or camera and film
Pictures of activities
Adult scissors
Tag board
Pencil
Ruler
Resealable plastic bags (sandwich size)
Stapler and staples

SKILL EXPLANATION:
An appreciation of literacy is advanced through the use of oral expression in association with a wordless book of pictures.

ADULT PREPARATION:
1. Make sure there is a copy of the permission form on file for each child to be photographed (Appendix B3).
2. Take and print pictures of activities throughout the day, from arrival to dismissal.
3. Use a pencil, ruler, and scissors to measure and cut a 14" × 7" piece of tag board.
4. Lay 10–12 resealable plastic sandwich bags on top of each other. Have all the resealable sections facing the right.

continued

Zipper Bag Story continued

5. Fold the tag board section in half, lengthwise.

6. Open the fold and place the left-hand section of the resealable bags in the center of the fold.

7. Fold the tagboard section closed.

8. Staple the tagboard and bags together securely.

9. Insert a picture into each baggie in the order of the day.

ACTIVITY INTRODUCTION SUGGESTION:

"We have a special book today about your school. This book is not written paper. It is pictures in baggies. Look at each picture and say what is going on in the picture."

THEME INTRODUCTION SUGGESTION:

"Our unit is *my school*." Show the zipper bag book. "We will tell a story from the pictures in this book."

PROCEDURES:

The child will complete the following steps:

1. Turn the pages of the zipper bag book.

2. Tell a story from the pictures, identifying the people in the pictures.

Zoo Adventures

SKILL EXPLANATION:

An appreciation of literacy and print awareness will be developed as the children listen to a book and then watch the adult write down a story they dictate.

ADULT PREPARATION:

1. Select a zoo book to read.

ACTIVITY INTRODUCTION SUGGESTION:

"What kind of animals are at the zoo? Today we will read a story about the zoo, and then you will be able to tell your own zoo story."

THEME INTRODUCTION SUGGESTION:

"Our unit is *the zoo*. If we traveled to the zoo, what animals would we see? Today we will read about the zoo and then we will make up our own zoo adventure."

PROCEDURES:

The children will complete the following steps:

1. Listen to the adult read the zoo book.
2. Take turns to look at the plastic zoo animals and dictate a story to the adult who writes it on plain paper.
3. Listen to the adult read the story that was dictated.
4. Draw a picture on the story page.

VARIATION:

Older children may not need to have the adult write down their dictation. If able, they may write their own story.

BOOK SUGGESTIONS:

* *Curious George Visits the Zoo* by Margaret Rey and Alan J. Shalleck (Boston, MA: Houghton Mifflin Company, 1985). As George is visiting the zoo, he had the opportunity to rescue a balloon for a child from the monkey's cage.
* *Zoo-Looking* by Mem Fox, illustrated by Candace Whitman. (Greenvale, NY: Mondo Publishing, 1996). This book is done in collage and watercolor and contains a repetitive phrase that children would enjoy saying along with the text.

AGES: 3–6

GROUP SIZE:
1–12 children

DEVELOPMENTAL GOALS:
* To promote oral expression
* To develop listening skills

LEARNING OBJECTIVE:
Using a zoo book and plastic zoo animals, the children will dictate an adventure at the zoo.

MATERIALS:
Zoo book
Plastic zoo animals
Plain paper
Pen or pencil
Colored pencils, crayons, or markers

References and Activities Book List

Addams, P. (2004). *Old MacDonald had a farm.* Auburn, ME: Child's Play.

Agee, J. (2001). *Milo's hat trick.* New York: Hyperion Books for Children.

American Heritage Dictionaries. (2007). *Picture dictionary.* New York: Houghton Mifflin Company.

Archambault, J. (2004). *Boom chicka rock.* New York: Scholastic, Inc.

Asch, F. (1979). *Popcorn.* New York: Parent's Magazine Press.

Bailer, B. (2005). *A B C animals: A bedtime story.* New York: Little Simon, 2005.

Bourgeois, P. (1987). *Big Sarah's little boots.* New York: Scholastic, Inc.

Brett, J. (2004). *The umbrella.* New York: G.P. Putnam's Sons.

Brown, M. (1996). *Arthur writes a story.* New York: Little, Brown & Co.

Brumbeau, J. (2004). *The quiltmaker's journey.* New York: Orchard Books.

Capucilli, A. S. (1995). *Inside a barn in the country.* New York: Scholastic.

Carle, E. (1993). *Today is Monday.* New York: Scholastic, Inc.

Carlstrom, N. W. (1986). *Jesse Bear, what will you wear?* New York: Simon & Schuster.

Carlstrom, N. W. (1992). *How do you say it today, Jesse Bear?* New York: Scholastic, Inc.

Cohen, M. (1967). *Will I have a friend?* New York: Scholastic, Inc.

Cronin, D. (2003). *Diary of a worm.* New York: Scholastic, Inc.

de Paola, T. (1985). *Mother goose.* New York: G.P. Putnam's Sons.

de Paola, T. (1988). *The legend of the Indian paintbrush.* New York: Putnam.

de Paola, T. (1991). *Pancakes.* New York: Scholastic.

Dobkin, B. (1993). *I love fishing.* Chicago: Children's Press.

Dr. Seuss. (1960). *Green eggs and ham.* New York: Random House.

Emery, D. (1975). *Teach your preschooler to read.* New York: Simon & Schuster.

Fleming, D. (2002). *Alphabet under construction.* New York: Henry Holt & Co.

Fox, M. (1996). *Zoo-looking.* Greenvale, NY: Mondo Publishing.

Galdone, P. (1973). *The three billy goats gruff.* New York: Clarion Books.

Gerstein, M. (2003). *The man who walked between the towers.* Brookfield, CT: Roaring Brook Press.

Granowsky, A. (2001). *Colors*. Brookfield, CT: Copper Beech Books.

Hennessy, B. G. (1989). *The missing tarts*. New York: Viking Penguin, Inc.

Hennessy, B. G. (1996). *Olympics!* New York: Penguin Group.

Hoban, T. (1983). *I read signs*. New York: Greenwillow Books.

Hoberman, M. A. (2003). *The lady with the alligator purse*. New York: Little, Brown, & Co.

Jarrie, M. (2005). *ABC USA*. New York: Sterling Publishing Co., Inc.

Jensen, E. (2004). *Brain compatible strategies*. San Diego, CA: The Brain Store.

Joffe, L. (1985). *If you give a mouse a cookie*. New York: Harper & Row.

Johnston, T. (1985). *The quilt story*. New York: Putman.

Johnston, T. (2003). *Go track a yak*. New York: Simon & Schuster Books for Young Readers.

Kalan, R. (1995). *Jump, frog, jump!* New York: Greenwillow Books.

Lansky, B. (2004). *Mary had a little jam and other silly rhymes*. New York: Meadowbrook Press.

LaRochelle, D. (2004). *The best pet of all*. New York: Dutton Children's Books.

Leedy, L. (1990). *The furry news: How to make a newspaper*. New York: Holiday House.

Lenski, L. (1962). *The little auto*. New York: Random House, 1962.

Lewis, R. (1999). *Friends*. New York: Henry Holt & Co.

Long, S. (1999). *Mother goose*. San Francisco: Chronicle Books.

Lyon, G. R. (1998, April 28). Overview of reading and literacy initiatives. *National Institute of Child Health & Human Development*. Retrieved July 27, 2006 from http://www.nichd.nih.gov

Maccarone, G. (1994). *Pizza party!* New York: Scholastic, Inc.

Marshall, J. (1988). *Goldilocks and the three bears*. New York: Dial.

Martin, B. (1967). *Brown bear, brown bear, what do you see?* New York: Henry Holt & Co.

McBratney, S. (2001). *I'll always be your friend*. HarperCollins Publishers.

McCloskey, R. (1948). *Blueberries for Sal*. New York: Viking Penguin, Inc.

McCloskey, R. (1940). *Lentil*. New York: The Viking Press.

McPhail, D. (1990). *Pig Pig gets a job*. New York: Dutton Children's Books.

Milhous, K. (1950). *The egg tree*. New York: Atheneum Books for Young Readers.

Moss, M. (1999). *Take a walk on a rainbow: A first look at color*. Minneapolis, Minnesota: Picture Window Books.

Most, B. (1978). *If the dinosaurs came back*. San Diego, CA: Harcourt, Inc.

Namm, D. (2004). *Pick a pet*. New York: Children's Press.

Neitzel, S. (2002). *Our class took a trip to the zoo*. New York: Greenwillow Books.

O'Callahan, J. (1992). *Tulips*. Atlanta, GA: Peachtree Publishers.

Pinczes, E. J. (1993). *One hundred hungry ants*. Boston: Houghton Mifflin Company.

Prince, J. (2006). *I saw an ant on the railroad track*. New York: Sterling Publishing Co., Inc.

Prosek, J. (2004). *A good day's fishing*. New York: Simon & Schuster.

Rey, M. (1958). *Curious George flies a kite*. Boston: Houghton Mifflin Company.

Rey, M., & Shalleck, A. J. (1985). *Curious George visits the zoo*. Boston: Houghton Mifflin Company.

Rice, E. (1981). *Benny bakes a cake*. New York: Greenwillow Books.

Rockwell, A. (2000). *Career day*. HarperCollins Publishers.

Rylant, C. (1985). *The relatives came*. New York: Bradbury Press.

Schiller, P., & Phipps, P. (2002). *The complete daily curriculum*. Beltsville, MD: Gryphon House.

Sendak, M. (1962). *Alligators all around*. New York: HarperCollins.

Sendak, M. (1963). *Where the wild things are*. New York: HarperCollins Children's Books.

Sharmat, M. (1980). *Gregory, the terrible eater*. New York: Scholastic, Inc.

Slate, J. (1996). *Miss Bindergarten gets ready for kindergarten*. New York: Scholastic, Inc.

Slobodkina, E. (1947). *Caps for sale*. New York: W.R. Scott.

Smith, J. A., & Read, S. (2005). *Early literacy instruction: A comprehensive framework for teaching reading and writing, K-3*. Upper Saddle River, New Jersey: Pearson.

Suen, A. (2003). *Raise the roof!* New York: Viking.

Taback, S. (2004). *Simms Taback's big book of words*. Maplewood, NJ: Blue Apple Books.

Thompson, L. (2004). *Little Quack's hide and seek*. New York: Simon & Schuster Books for Young Readers.

Vonk, I. (1983). *Storytelling with the flannel board*. Minneapolis, MN: T.S. Denison & Company, Inc.

Yorinks, A. (1986). *Hey Al!* New York: Farrar, Straus and Giroux.

Wagner, K. (1998). *A friend like Ed*. New York: Scholastic, Inc.

Wells, R. (1999). *Bingo*. New York: Scholastic Press.

Wiesner, D. (1991). *Tuesday*. New York: Clarion Books.

Williams, S. (1989). *I went walking*. New York: Trumpet Club.

Wood, A. (1990). *Weird Parents*. New York: Puffin Books.

Wright, G. F. (1916). *The real mother goose*. Chicago: Rand McNally & Company.

Zolotow, C. (2003). *Hold my hand: Five stories of love and family*. New York: Hyperion Books for Children.

Appendix A: Activities Patterns

A1. ALLIGATOR

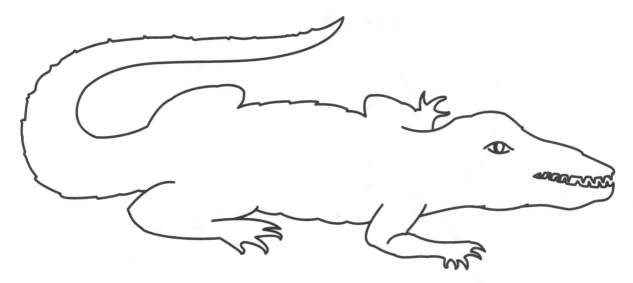

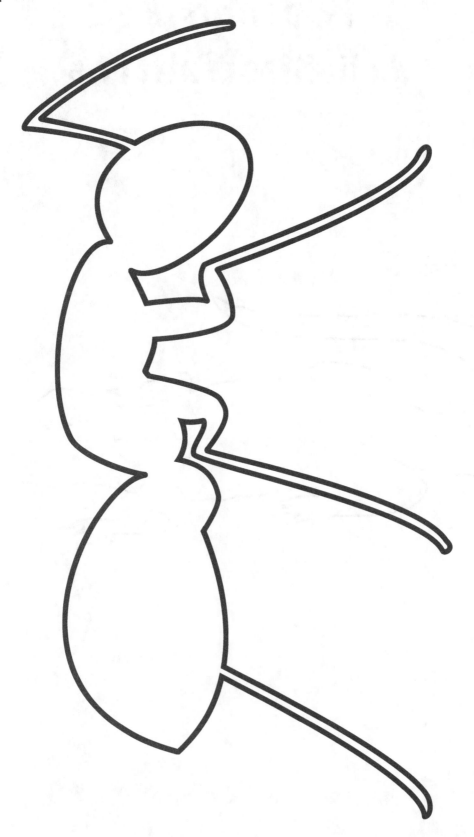

A3. FISH

A4. BRIDGE

A5. BARN

A6. RIVER

A7. GREAT GRUFF GOATS

continued

A9. ICE

A10. MICE

A11. MITTEN

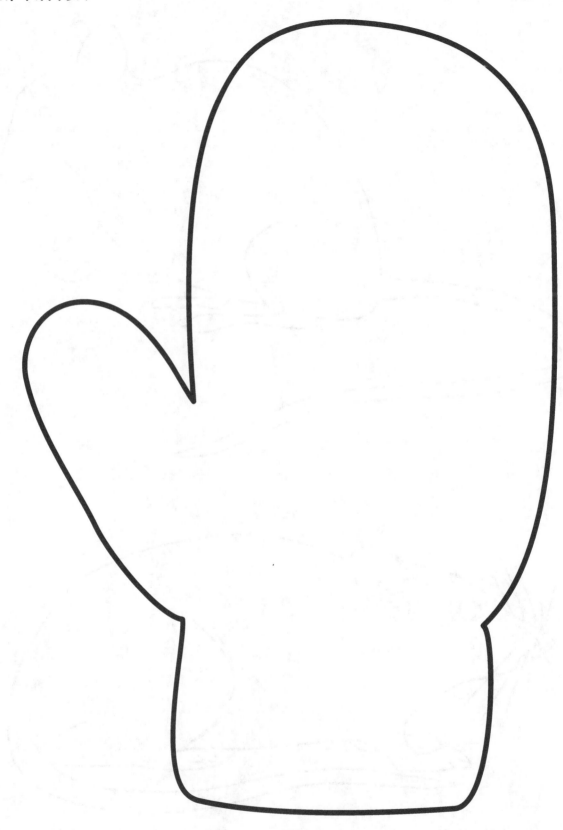

A12. KITTEN

A13. HAT

A14. CAT

A15. COAT

A16. BOAT

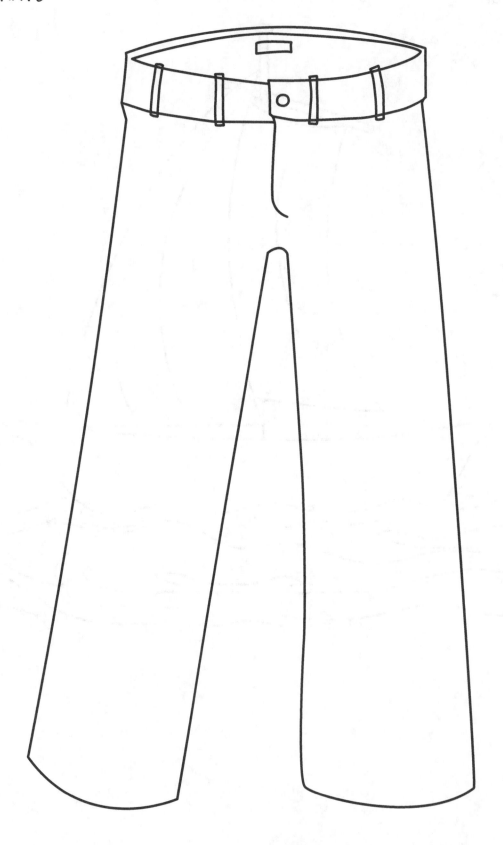

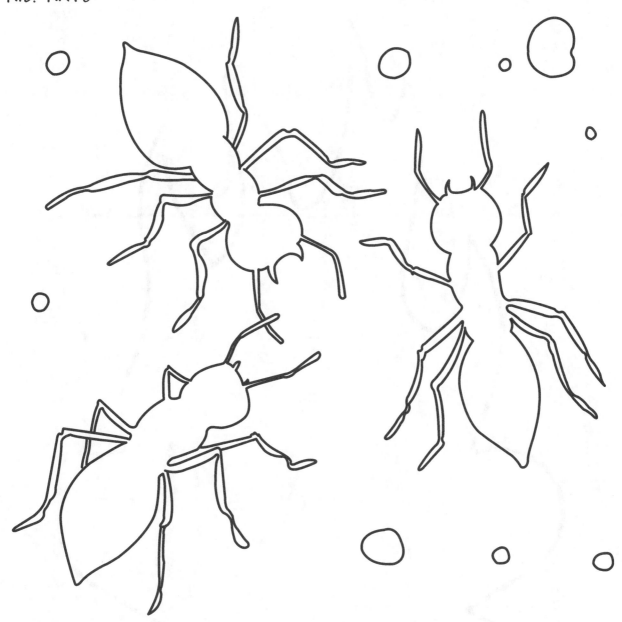

A19. FIRE

A20. TIRE

A21. CAR

A22. KEY

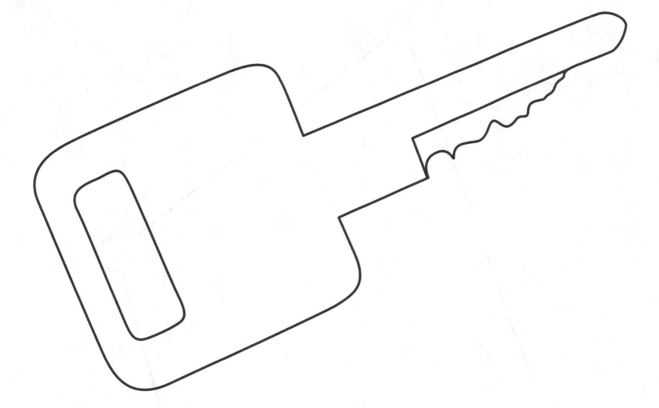

A23. KITE

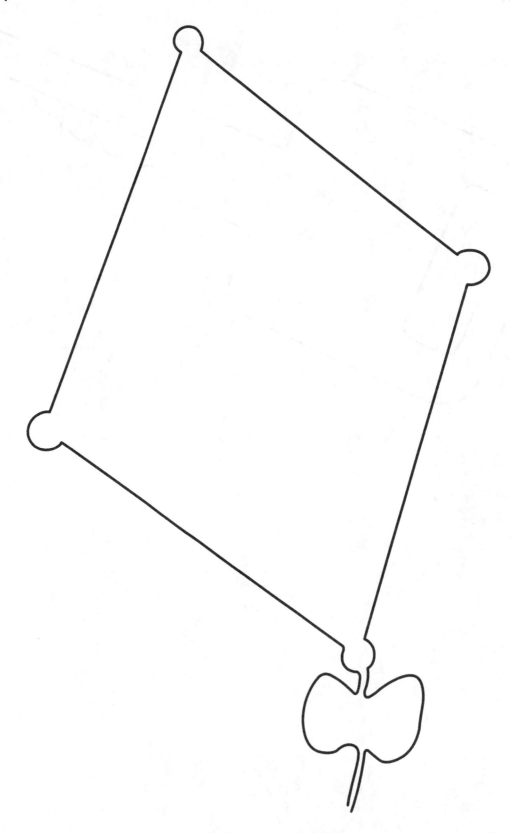

A24. JACK BE NIMBLE

A25. RUB-A DUB-DUD, THREE MEN IN A TUB

A26. JACK AND JILL

A27. LITTLE BOY BLUE COME BLOW YOUR HORN

A28. CROWN

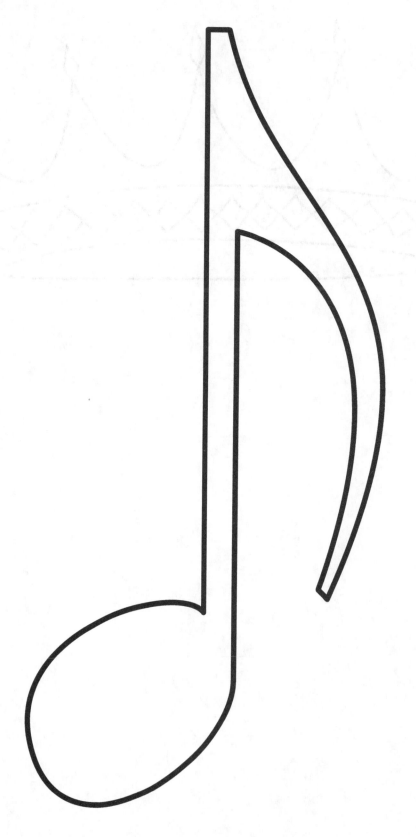

A30. TRUCK

A31. VAN

A32. BUS

A33. JEEP

A34. APPLE

A35. GATE

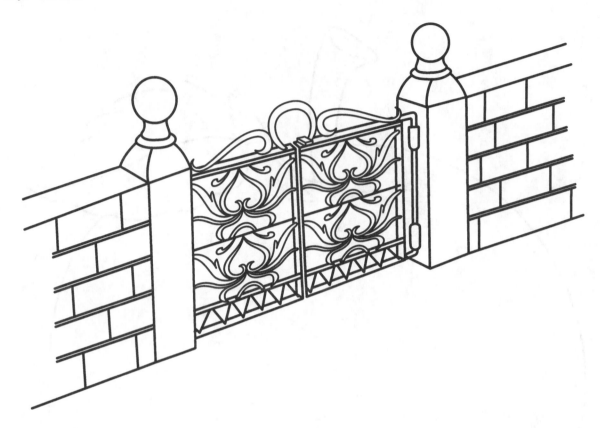

A36. EGG

A37. BEE

A38. IGUANA

A39. OSTRICH

A40. SUN

A41. MULE

A42. WORM

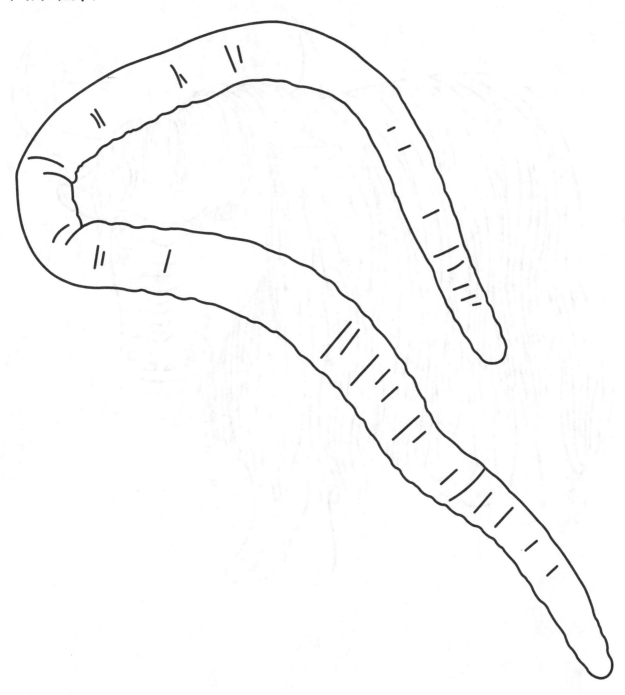

A43. YAK

Appendix B

B1. Dolch words (high frequency words). Words are given in order of frequency. B1 is also used with 7 other activities such as: *Everlasting Puffy Paint, Fishy Words, Hide and Seek High Frequencey Words, Key Words, Magnetic Word Match, Shaving Cream Writing, and Vocabulary Building Blocks.*

1. the	2. to	3. and	4. he	5. a
6. I	7. you	8. it	9. of	10. in
11. was	12. said	13. his	14. that	15. she
16. for	17. on	18. they	19. but	20. had
21. at	22. him	23. with	24. up	25. all
26. look	27. is	28. her	29. there	30. some
31. out	32. as	33. be	34. have	35. go
36. we	37. am	38. then	39. little	40. down
41. do	42. can	43. could	44. when	45. did
46. what	47. so	48. see	49. not	50. were
51. get	52. them	53. like	54. one	55. this
56. my	57. would	58. me	59. will	60. yes
61. big	62. went	63. are	64. come	65. if
66. now	67. long	68. no	69. came	70. ask
71. very	72. an	73. over	74. your	75. its
76. ride	77. into	78. just	79. blue	80. red
81. from	82. good	83. any	84. about	85. around
86. want	87. don't	88. how	89. know	90. right
91. put	92. too	93. got	94. take	95. where

96. every	97. pretty	98. jump	99. green	100. four
101. away	102. old	103. by	104. their	105. here
106. saw	107. call	108. after	109. well	110. think
111. ran	112. let	113. help	114. make	115. going
116. sleep	117. brown	118. yellow	119. five	120. six
121. walk	122. two	123. or	124. before	125. eat
126. again	127. play	128. who	129. been	130. may
131. stop	132. off	133. never	134. seven	135. eight
136. cold	137. today	138. fly	139. myself	140. round
141. tell	142. much	143. keep	144. give	145. work
146. first	147. try	148. new	149. must	150. start
151. black	152. white	153. ten	154. does	155. bring
156. goes	157. write	158. always	159. drink	160. once
161. soon	162. made	163. run	164. gave	165. open
166. has	167. find	168. only	169. us	170. three
171. our	172. better	173. hold	174. buy	175. funny
176. warm	177. ate	178. full	179. those	180. done
181. use	182. fast	183. say	184. light	185. pick
186. hurt	187. pull	188. cut	189. kind	190. both
191. sit	192. which	193. fall	194. carry	195. small
196. under	197. read	198. why	199. own	200. found
201. wash	202. show	203. hot	204. because	205. far
206. live	207. draw	208. clean	209. grow	210. best
211. upon	212. these	213. sing	214. together	215. please
216. thank	217. wish	218. many	219. shall	220. laugh

B2. Family Letter 1

Date:

Dear Family,

I have brought home a bag of word cards. I can practice identifying the cards and then pairing two words together to make a sentence. Together we could also copy these words on separate index cards. Then I could practice matching words between the two sets.

Love,

B3. Permission form to be photographed and videotaped

My child, _____ has permission to be photographed or videotaped for educational purposes and/or class activities while attending _____ _____
(Child care center or school).

Parent's signature _____

Date _____

B4. Family Letter 2

Date:

Dear Family,

I have written a secret message to you on this sheet of white paper. Please iron it on low heat and the message will appear.

Love,

B5. Family Letter 3

Date:

Dear Family,

It's my turn to bring the letter bag to school. We need to look around the house and find things that start with the letter _____. We will put the items in the bag and bring it to school on our next school day. At school we will identify each item and note that they began with the letter of the week. At the end of the day, I will bring the bag and our items home.

Love,

quarter	
quail	
queen	
quill	
quilt	

■ sat on the □.

■ is on the □.

■ is in the □.

■ has a □.

Where is ■?

B8. Family Letter 4

Date:

Dear Family,

It's my turn to bring (*pet's name*) home this weekend. At the end of the weekend we are to write in the journal, telling what (*pet's name*) did and where he went this weekend.

Love,

Appendix C: Handwriting Styles of Manuscript Print

C1. D'NEALIAN

Mod Manuscript

ABCDEFGHIJ

KLMNOPQRST

UVWXYZabcdef

ghijklmnopqrstuv

wxyz123456789

0

Mod Cursive

ABCDEFGHI

JKLMNOPQR

STUVWXYZ

abcdefghijklmno

pqrstuvwxyz12

3456789

Palmer

ABCDEFGHIJ
KLMNOPQRS
TUVWXYZabc
defghijklmnopqrs
tuvwxyz123456
7890

Palmer

ABCDEFG
HIJKLMNO
PQRSTUV
WXYZabcdef
ghijklmnopq
rstuvwxyz12

ABCDEFGHIJ
KLMNOPQRST
UVWXYZabcde
fghijklmnopqrstu
VWXYZ1234567890

ABCDEFGHIJKL
MNOPQRSTUVW
XYZabcdefghijkl
mmopqrstuvwx
yz1234567890

Manuscript-simple
ABCDEFGHIJ
KLMNOPQRS
TUVWXYZabcd
efghijklmnopqrstu
vwxyz1234567890

Manuscript
ABCDEFGHIJK
LMNOPQRSTU
VWXYZabcdefg
hijklmnopqrstuvw
xyz1234567890

Cursive simple
ABCDEF GH
IJKLMNOP
QRSTUVWXY
Zabcdefghijklm
nopqrstuvwxyz
1234567890

ABCDEF GH
IJKLMNO
PQRSTUV
WXYZabcdefgh
ijklmnopqrstu
nvwxyz123456

Appendix D

D1. Doggie, Doggie, Where's Your Bone Rebus Chant?

, , where's your ?

🚶 took it from your 🏠.

D2. Doggie, Doggie, Where's Your Bone Rebus Recipe

1. Wash 🖐️.

2. Put ½ 🥤 of 🛍️ into a 🥣.

3. Put ⅛ 🥤 of 🥫 into the 🥣.

4. Stir 🥣.

5. Mold 🦴.

6. Place 🦴 on a 🍽️.

7. Write name .

8. ⬜ for 30 ⬜.

D3. Frozen Fruit Pops
Rebus Recipe

1. Wash 🖐.

2. Put 2 🥄 of 🍉 in
the 🥤.

3. Put 2 🍉 of 🧃 in
the 🥤.

4. Stir the 🍉 and 🧃.

5. Place a 🥄 in the 🥤.

6. Place the 🥤 on a
tray.

7. Place in the 🧊.

D4. Rebus Recipe for Toast Writing

1. Wash 🖐.

2. Put on a 👕.

3. Put 🥛 🥛 into a 🥛.

4. Put 4 💧 of 🍶 into the 🥛.

5. Stir the 🥣 with a 🥄.

6. Put 🍞 on a ⭕.

7. Use the 🥄 to ✍️.

8. Set the on the .

9. .

10. for 5 .

D5. Rebus Recipe for Wild Thing Snack

1. Wash 🤲.

2. 🥣 cream cheese.

3. Add 🍇 for 👁 👁.

4. Add 🍓 for 👄.

5. Add 🍚 for 💇 and 🧔.

Theme Index

Index